Resolis

"Slope of Light"

Guide to a Black Isle Parish

Two
Triangular Carved Wallstones,
similarly designed with fleur-de-lis and scrolls, 17ᵗʰ century.
Top: Braelangwell, initials of Master Thomas Urquhart with Urquhart boar heads.
Bottom: West Brae, built into successive houses to mark location of the Old House of Brae.

Resolis

"Slope of Light"

Guide to a Black Isle Parish

Dr Jim Mackay

iii

Published in Great Britain, 2009, by:

Jim Mackay
Firichean House
Cullicudden
Dingwall
Scotland IV7 8LL

British Library Cataloguing-in-Publication Data
A catalogue record for this book is available from the British Library.

ISBN 978-0-9562102-0-3

Typeset by Jim Mackay.
Printed and bound by A4 Design & Print Ltd, Inverness.

Funding support from Resolis Community Council, the Highland Council and the Kirkmichael Trust is acknowledged with thanks. Profits from sales will go to the Kirkmichael Trust, which seeks to restore the Kirkmichael site in Resolis for public benefit; for information see the Trust's website: www.kirkmichael.info

PREFACE

Resolis, the northernmost Black Isle parish, is rich in historical incident and both built and natural heritage interest. Its pastoral beauty, set against the dramatic back-drop of the Sutors, the Cromarty Firth, the Ardross Hills, Ben Wyvis and the hills to the west, is a resource to be cherished.

It was formed from two earlier parishes, Kirkmichael and Cullicudden. The Gaelic name *"Resolis,"* meaning *"Bright Slope"* or *"Slope of Light,"* originally applied to the small settlement in the centre of the parish where the new church was built, but gradually became applied to the united parish. Resolis is now part of a wider parish itself. In a civil context, the parish was absorbed into the larger District of Black Isle (North). In a religious context, it is now united with other parishes. However, in a community context, Resolis flourishes with Resolis Primary School, Resolis Memorial Hall and the many Resolis community groups providing a clear local identity.

Resolis has been subject to constant change. Short agricultural tenancies resulted in few families staying in place for more than a generation. Estates swelled and diminished with the fortunes of their owners. Tenants' homes, some estate houses and even a castle have disappeared into the turf, and locations of an astonishing number of schools and churches are dotted around the parish. Ferries and tracks were supplanted by bridges and improved roads. Many of the residents who would once have gained a living from the land now commute to work in Easter Ross or Inverness or are being replaced by those seeking an idyllic country home retiral.

Change in the parish is inevitable. The challenge is to seize the best opportunities to enhance the parish and to reject those that do not. It is hoped that by adding to the appreciation of the heritage of the parish, this small book can assist that process.

––––––––––

I was delighted to be requested to produce this guide to the parish. The first half is thematic (natural history, education, religion, crime and so on). The second half is a gazetteer, in which all natural, architectural and historical features of interest are described. Those who attended my lectures on the history of the parish some years ago will know that I love a good story, and here I have inserted many colourful (but true) incidents.

Previous guidebooks have perpetuated errors in relation to Resolis, such as the mythical *"Jemima Poyntz"* and the incorrect meaning of *"Ellan Vannin."* I have strived to eliminate these through research in original source material, but errors do creep in, so let me know if you spot any. Queries on location of specific source material, corrections or provision of further information will all be welcomed and can be directed to me at the address on the facing page.

DEDICATION

To my wife Carlann and my children Kirsty and Gavin.

ACKNOWLEDGEMENTS

I am indebted to:

Andrew Dowsett, Scoulag, for the photographs taken by himself of the Lady Ardoch mausoleum, the Grant of Ardoch mausoleum, the Kirkmichael guided tour, the Kirkmichael medieval cross and the big bales and oil rig scene on the inside cover.
Catriona Gillies, North Kessock, for the photograph of Scott's taxi on her grandfather's Ferry-boat at Balblair and for allowing me to reproduce the portion of *"View of Poyntzfield, Bay of Cromarty"* by J R Thompson on the inside cover.
James Holm, Ferryton, for the cover photograph of the Newhall School gardening class of 1922.
Sheila Macdonald, Avoch, for photographs of her father's traction engine at Newmills and his mobile mill at Gordon's Mill.
Angus Mackenzie, Caladh, Newton of Ferintosh, for the cover photograph of *"Cocoa-Hour"* at Cullicudden School *c*1914.
Essie Munro, previously of Alness Ferry and now of Avoch, for the photographs of Kirkmichael in *c*1906 and Kinbeachie Castle.
Donny Munro, Newhall Bridge, for permission to reproduce extracts of the works of his grandfather, Angus Munro, Newhall Bridge.

All modern photography, except where identified otherwise, is by the author.

CONTENTS

Three Bridges from the abandoned Light Railway.

Above: Newmills, over the mill lade at NH67336480.
Left: Jemimaville, over the Udale Burn at NH72106525.
Below: Braelangwell's *"Bridge to Nowhere"* over the Braelangwell Burn at NH69406488.

VITAL STATISTICS

Resolis lies on the south coast of the Cromarty Firth, running 11 km parallel to the Firth and reaching 5 km inland at its widest. It rises from sea-level to the summit of Mount Eagle, the highest point of the Black Isle, at 256 m.

The parishes bounding Resolis are Cromarty to the east, Urquhart and Logie Wester to the west, Avoch and Rosemarkie to the south and, across the Firth, Kiltearn, Alness and Rosskeen. Resolis itself was created in 1662 from the separate parishes of Kirkmichael and Cullicudden; Resolis, although used in the civil context as the parish name, was more formally used in a church context as *"The united parish of Kirkmichael & Cullicudden, commonly known as Resolis."*

There were three ferries servicing Resolis, Invergordon-Balblair (the most important, and originally known as the Inverbreakie Ferry), Alness-Alness Ferry and Foulis Ferry, landing at least latterly at Toberchurn. The name of Ferryton suggests a fourth. Early roads crossed the high moors of the Millbuie to connect these Cromarty Firth ferries to the ferries to the south at Fortrose and Kessock, the most important connection being from Balblair to Kessock via Agneshill and Auchterflow. Another early track ran the length of the parish, connecting up the ferry tracks with Cromarty.

An inn or a shop lay close to each ferry point– Balblair Ferry Inn and several shops at Balblair, various shops at Resolis crossroads above Alness Ferry, an inn and shop at Bruichglass above the Foulis Ferry. There were other inns, one at Drumcudden (present day Ellan Vannin), another at Birks and at least one in Jemimaville (known as the Plough Inn and then the Poyntzfield Arms). And there were many other shops, some ephemeral like Barnetson's at Auchmartin (1936-1956), some associated with other enterprises like St Martins Smiddy and the Post Offices, and some long-established, as in Jemimaville. There are at present no ferries, inns or shops in Resolis, but there is still one small Post Office in Jemimaville and of course there is still a Smiddy operating at Newhall Bridge.

The highest recorded population figure was 1,568 (1861), the lowest 524 (1971) and the most recent 736 (2001). Jemimaville, established in 1822, is the only village of any scale. Other centres of population include Bablair, Newhall, Mount High, Chapelton, Craigton, Newmills and Gordon's Mill. Some of the side roads conceal a surprising number of modern houses. A planning application for a new village near Mount High granted planning permission in recent years at time of writing had not yet been implemented.

Resolis falls nowadays within the school catchment of Fortrose Academy, although pupils in the past also attended Dingwall and Invergordon Academies. There is one primary school in Resolis. It opened to pupils in 2007 and provides many community facilities. There is also the splendid Resolis Memorial Hall, which has served the community well since 1959.

THE LAND

The solid geology of Resolis is without exception middle Old Red Sandstone. The Millbuie Ridge is one of a series of north east – south west-trending folds in the Old Red Sandstone which have weathered out into a number of parallel ridges and valleys. This repeated fall and rise of the landscape in Resolis is experienced on the descent from the Millbuie to the Firth, with burns, tracks and roads all running parallel with the geology.

The Old Red Sandstone of the Black Isle has been much quarried as masonry stone. The remains of at least five quarries and their spoilheaps can be seen along the Resolis shoreline. These have all been partly filled with cultivation stones and other debris, but the largest (at Wester Cullicudden) with its pier, by means of which the stone was shipped, still survives. Cullicudden stone can be found in many buildings in the North of Scotland, such as the first Cromarty Free Church and the Coul House Hotel in Contin.

The drift geology is glacial till (once known, more descriptively, as boulder clay) deposited by the process of glaciation at various depths over bedrock. The glacial till, while having a high clay content, also contains variable proportions of sand, pebbles and boulders of sometimes substantial dimensions.

Pockets of high clay content glacial till were sought out locally and excavated for use in building tenants' houses and steadings. For example, there are two dips in the brae faces at Alness Ferry known to be the sources of the clay forming the matrix around the rough stones of the buildings in the locality.

Hundreds of wells were sunk through the glacial till until water was struck. From first edition Ordnance Survey mapping (1870s), it can be seen that every farmstead distant from a burn had its own water supply.

The soils in Resolis, as across the Black Isle, are humus-iron podzols formed on fluvioglacial drift derived from the Old Red Sandstone and from raised beach deposits. Much of the land is capable of quality arable production, but this should not obscure the work that much of it required through stone clearance, rectification of acidity and natural deficiencies in elements such as cobalt and copper, breaking up the sometimes concrete-like iron pan at the interface of

Wells along the Cullicudden Straight.

topsoil and subsoil, and installation of drainage (stone drains being replaced by clay pipe drains being in turn supplanted by perforated plastic piping).

Across much of Resolis, only topsoil that has been worked for many years is free from stones. Indeed, relative freedom from stones could be used as a parameter for assessing when arable cultivation began. Moors freshly brought into cultivation look more like quarries than fields when the plough succeeds in turning the turf partially over. No matter how many stones are gathered in one year, the next cold spring brings an undiminished fresh crop.

These stones have sometimes been carried by glaciers a considerable distance. One study showed the location of three Inchbae augen gneiss erratics carried about 30 km from their distinctive source to their destination in the boulder clay in Resolis. Other stones were carried much further.

Raised beaches, present all around the Black Isle to varying degree, are prominent along most of the coastline of Resolis. These are well-marked terraces, where the soil above and below the former cliffs contains pebbles rounded by the action of the sea. Land rose in several stages when the vast weight of ice on Scotland melted at the end of the last Ice Age. Scotland is still slowly rising from the sea, although sea level is predicted to rise rapidly from the impact of global warming, so the lower raised beaches of Resolis may disappear once again into the sea.

Field clearance stones used to create track and coast protection, Alness Ferry; raised beaches behind.

FAUNA, FLORA, FARMING AND FORESTRY

The moorland of Resolis has been progressively turned into agricultural or forestry land. Estate plans from 18th and 19th centuries (many of which survive) demonstrate a patchwork of small areas of active agricultural land set within a matrix of moorland (used for common grazing), bogs and lochs.

Agricultural improvement over the 18th, 19th and 20th centuries has resulted in the reverse: a few areas of moorland or bog set in mostly intensively managed agricultural land or forestry plantation. It would be appropriate now to maintain the little that is left. The few remaining patches of birch woodland in the parish have been unsympathetically treated as ready-made landscaping for new housing development instead of a valued habitat.

Much tree planting, associated both with estate amenity and commercial enterprise, was carried out in the late 18th – mid 19th centuries. And following the formation of the Forestry Commission in 1919, large-scale afforestation began in the Black Isle, including considerable areas on higher ground in Resolis, obliterating many farmsteads in Agneshill, and the heavy cultivation equipment damaging the prehistoric burial grounds on the higher ground. However, the Forestry Commission was an important employer in the area and the settlement at Mount High originated as housing for forestry workers.

The intertidal areas within Resolis, stretching along the coastline of the Black Isle, and including the extensive mud flats of Udale Bay, are contained within a Site of Special Scientific Interest (national), Special Protection Area (European) and Ramsar (international) site. Further out to sea are areas with the European designation of Special Areas of Conservation. Much of Udale Bay is also a National Nature Reserve. Udale Bay is part of an area of Shellfish Growing

Udale Bay from Chapelton; the Sutors behind.

Waters and just to the east of Jemimaville there is a much greater Shellfish Production Area, both designated by the Scottish Government. All of these were designated relatively recently, indicating how lately the natural interests of the area have become appreciated.

Braelangwell Wood Site of Special Scientific Interest, centred on NH688632, a 68.2 ha site, was first notified in 1974. It is described as one of the few surviving areas of semi-natural woodland on the Black Isle and also as one of only a handful of areas in Easter Ross where calcareous springs emanating from the Old Red Sandstone Rocks survive unmodified. These calcium rich springs have given rise to a flora and invertebrate community of considerable interest.

Farmland at Wood of Brae beside the semi-natural woodland of the SSSI.

From the hide near Jemimaville, the vast numbers of wildfowl and waders such as wigeon, mallard, godwit, heron, goldeneye, teal, dunlin and grey knot can be seen on the intertidal sand and mud flats at Udale Bay, flocking and feeding.

Udale Bay is now an RSPB Reserve, but there are memories from the 1930s of the birds on Udale Bay providing an income – a local would lie on his back at night on a punt waiting with a punt gun for the ducks to come over. The punt gun was lit by a fuse, and when it would go off the whole of the Bay would be illuminated. The ducks that were still more or less in one piece were sold to a butcher in Invergordon for 1/6 for a good bird, and with a bag of sometimes 30-40 birds in a night, it could be a worthwhile enterprise.

Pine marten (hated by many local farmers) and wild cat are some of the rarer creatures which can be glimpsed within Resolis. Rabbit populations, on which so many predators are dependent, fluctuate dramatically. The wire remnants of rabbit snares can still be seen on the lower wires of old fences, as rabbit was once a common supplement to the Resolis diet.

Sage in 1836 wrote: "*Rabbits were introduced a few years ago, by a gentleman who had a temporary residence in this parish, and have now so much increased as to have become a public nuisance.*" Wild pigeon were eaten, caught by a variety of ingenious measures. There were also pigeon houses, or doocots, at Newhall, Braelangwell and Poyntzfield at least.

The hovering red kite has now become a commonplace sight since its recent re-introduction. Roe deer are common in the forestry, venturing out to farmland to graze, sometimes even reaching the Firth.

Pheasant are nowadays shot in the St Martins and Nutwood area to a limited extent, but shooting was once important to the estates. The 1918 Newhall Sale Particulars state: "*The Grouse Moor affords capital Shooting throughout the Season. It is easily walked and readily lends itself to driving. An average bag should include 80-100 brace of grouse; 10 black game; 150 brace of partridges, besides a varied bag of pheasants, snipe, woodcock, wild duck, plover, hares, and rabbits, with an occasional roe deer and capercailzie. Large quantities of duck and wildfowl frequent the Cromarty Firth and Newhall Bay.*"

Seals, dolphins and porpoises can be seen in the Firth, reflecting the ample supply of fish. Newhall and Poyntzfield Estates used stake-nets and yares to catch fish around Udale Bay. At Newhall-point in the 18th and 19th centuries, salmon stake nets were very successful, the fish being shipped south, kept cool with ice stored in the ice-house which still stands on the property now known as Scoulag. The enterprise was abolished by Parliament on the claim by Conon proprietors that it affected their enterprise, leaving Newhall with the right to bag net only, not often exercised. However, many of the crofters with land on the Firth continued to use an unauthorised conventional net, a practice not yet entirely extinct, the net being pulled in in the evening when activities cannot be spotted by the bailiffs across the Firth in Easter Ross.

The Newhall Estate icehouse at Scoulag; ice was shovelled in through the hatch.

ANCIENT HISTORY – IN BRIEF

The last withdrawal of the ice occurred in the area about 10,000 BC. Only about 5,000 BC do traces of mobile Mesolithic culture appear, in the coastal mounds of food remains or middens, several of which occur in the Black Isle. Neolithic man, the first farmer, arrived about 4,000 BC, and Resolis has examples of both his cairns and his chambered tombs (see page 9 and Gazetteer).

Evidence was uncovered in the 1990s at Kinbeachie Farm (centred round NH626625) of Neolithic human activity. Excavations revealed the post holes of a timber building about 7 m x 4 m, with several pits nearby containing incised potsherds and a miniature polished stone axe. A number of apparently isolated pits may be remains of structures damaged beyond recognition. Assemblages of flint and carbonised grain were also recovered. The finds associated with the timber structure indicate that it is Neolithic. Fieldwalking on the farm resulted in flint finds including a leaf-shaped arrowhead. A small pit contained charcoal which has been dated to 3,795-3,640 BC.

Around 2,500 BC, a decorated type of pottery is associated with burials – the so-called Beaker people have arrived, bringing with them skill in working copper and, in time, bronze. Also associated with the Bronze Age are the (presumably) religious monuments – cup-marked rocks, standing stones, stone circles, henges, no examples of which are found in Resolis, although examples of all but the stone circles are found in adjacent parishes or across the Firth.

The climate deteriorated in the late Bronze Age. With the Iron Age, about 700 BC, come the brochs, no examples of which are found in the Black Isle, and the duns, a ruined example of which is nearby at Culbokic. The domestic dwellings of this period remain the hut circles. Examples of the ornamented weapons and rich jewellery of the ruling families of this Age have survived.

The Romans made excursions into the North, clearly admiring the safety of the Cromarty Firth as a haven for they named it "*Portus Salutis,*" but they did not establish themselves on the Black Isle.

Pictish culture is first referred to by classical writers in the late 3rd century AD. The Pictish term "*pit*" for a parcel of land is common in the Black Isle. Pictish symbol stones and much later (9th century AD), more complex, Christian carvings, are found in and around the Black Isle, although not in Resolis itself. It is hypothesised that Christianity had spread to Ross and Cromarty by the end of the 7th century.

The many Viking place-names around the coasts of Britain indicate the migratory influence of the Vikings, mostly in the late 8th and 9th centuries. In Resolis, the names Culbo and the "*langwell*" part of Braelangwell are thought to be of Viking origin.

Early Christian religious teaching was initially based upon the monastery. The locations of some early churches can be identified from place-names beginning with "*Cill*" or "*Kil*" (monk's cell or church) as in Kilmuir or Kilmichael.

As the papal system developed, under the rule of Bishops, parishes and parish churches were established, with Cullicudden and Kirkmichael (later united into Resolis) formed perhaps in the 12th century. The earliest written reference to Cullicudden found so far is 1227; to Kirkmichael, 1429. The human remains found at the burial ground at Chapelton (Balblair) have been dated to a period *c*11th to *c*12th centuries, although no definite church remains were found. The focus of church life in the Black Isle was Fortrose Cathedral, some of the architecture of which is 14th century.

The earldom of Ross is referred to as early as the 12th century, and the earldom included land in modern Easter Ross and the north part of the Black Isle. The small but strategically important sheriffdom of Cromarty was probably established before 1300, but was added to by the work of the wily Sir George Mackenzie of Tarbat through the inclusion of his estates following Acts in 1685 and 1698, much of the estate of the Urquharts of Cromarty having been lost by debts to Tarbat. He became Earl of Cromartie in 1703. The 1685 Act of Parliament disjoined (in Resolis) "*the lands of Wester St. Martin's, Easter Belblair, and the ferry belonging to George Dallace of St. Martin's,*" from the sheriffdom of Ross, and annexed them to the sheriffdom of Cromartie.

Resolis falling within two shires led to an unusual defence in several legal proceedings. As recently as 1852, in Graham *v* Disher, the ingenious publican at Balblair Inn, James Graham, argued that the Court of Cromarty held no jurisdiction over him as the Inn fell within the County of Ross.

Medieval arched tomb recess at Kirkmichael; text on central stone undeciphered.

SCHEDULED MONUMENTS

A scheduled monument is an ancient monument of national importance which has been given legal protection under the Ancient Monuments and Archaeological Areas Act 1979. Site details are given in the Gazetteer. Scheduling seems somewhat haphazard – for example, the icehouse at Scoulag is similar to the scheduled icehouse at Helmsdale, the medieval Calvary crosses at Cullicudden are more remarkable than some of the scheduled stones elsewhere.

Prehistoric Ritual and Funerary
NH648595	Cnoc nan Craiseag, cairn, Mount Eagle
NH672661	Cnoc nan Taibhsean, cairn
NH661628	Easter Brae, long cairn and cairn
NH656613	Wester Brae, long cairn 650 m SSE of (photograph page 36)
NH650610	Woodhead, chambered cairn 350 m E of (photograph page 36)
NH653607	Woodhead, long cairn 600 m ESE of Woodhead Farm
NH713631	Upperwood, cairn 165 m SSE of

Prehistoric Domestic and Defensive
NH653617	Wester Brae, hut circles & field system

Secular
NH631638	Craig Castle, tower

Ecclesiastical
NH708670	Newhall Point, chapel and burial ground, Balblair
NH705658	St Michael's Church, Kirton

Left: quern found SW of the Corrie by George Mackay.
Above: axeheads found Auchmartin by James Ferguson
and flint tools found Alness Ferry by George Mackay.

MODERN HISTORY (1400s-present day)

THE PEOPLE

From the first population assessment in 1755 of 1,371, the population declined to a low point of 1,067 in 1801, but rose steadily again to the highest population of 1,568 in 1861. There was a long-term decline over the late 19th century and much of the 20th century, reaching a nadir in 1971 of only 524. Over more recent decades, the population has risen again and stood in 2001 at 736.

The pattern of increase and rural depopulation is the general one for the region. Some early fluctuations were explained by the Reverend Arthur in 1792: *"The decrease from 1780 to 1789, was occasioned, in a great measure, by the arrears of rent, and other debts unavoidably incurred by the tenants, through the failure of crop 1782, which obliged them, in 1783, to dismiss every servant they could possibly spare, and make their children endeavour to supply their places, at a much earlier period than they were wont to do before; and ever since that memorable era, many of the young and stoutest lads, have annually gone to Glasgow, and other places in the west and south of Scotland, where the price of labour is high, instead of marrying and settling in the parish, as was the custom formerly. This annual drain of young men, has raised the wages of servants, and is severely felt by the tenants."*

"The increase of population from 1789 to 1792, was owing to the great encouragement given by Mr. and Mrs. Urquhart of Braelangwell and Newhall to people who settled on, and improved moor-ground."

The difference between 1821 and 1831 was explained in the Session Records as due *"to the influx of Strangers into the Parish from two causes, viz (i) the*

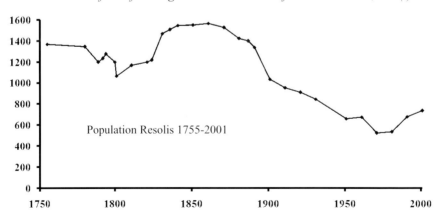

Population Resolis 1755-2001

cutting down two large fir woods, many of the labourers employed in which settled in the parish & (2d) A village established on the Estate of Geo. Gunn Munro Es^r of Poyntzfield in the year 1822 [Jemimaville] *& which has been annually increasing."*

In 1824, 55% of the Resolis population were recorded as being habitual Gaelic speakers. In 1881 42% Gaelic speakers are recorded. In 1891, a useful distinction in these statistics was made – 44% could speak both Gaelic and English, and 1% Gaelic only. In 1901, 39% were bilingual, and less than 0.5% spoke only Gaelic. From the Census records, Gaelic tended to be associated with poorer families and the many families who moved into Resolis from the West.

These detailed Census returns (1841 onwards) show over the 19th century that a significant proportion of the Resolis population was born on the West Coast (Gairloch, Lochcarron, Lochbroom, etc.) These were families, dispossessed through either poverty or the actions of landowners, being encouraged by the Resolis estate owners to settle upon their estates (thereby speeding the process of agricultural improvement).

FAMILY NAMES

In the ten year period July 1748-June 1758, from 402 children baptised, the ten commonest family names in the parish were McKenzie (11%), Fraser, Urquhart, Holm, Murray, Munro, Grant, Hossack, Ferguson and Forbes (3%). One hundred years later, from the 1,550 people in the 1851 Census, the ten commonest names had changed to McKenzie (10%), MacDonald, Fraser, Urquhart, Munro, Holm, Cameron, Ross, McLennan and McKay (3%).

At both times, there was a plethora of less common family names, including much evidence of the use of the patronymic "*alias*" (supposed old family name). Records such as "*Donald McDonald alias Caundach*" present a particular problem to family historians. Christian Cameron in 1834 successfully obtained a formal amendment to the 1796 Resolis baptism register. She protested that: "*the real surname of her & of her brother's family and forefathers is Cameron, but that from the first of them who came to reside in this Country they Received the patronimick Surname of Mackiddy.*"

INDUSTRIES AND OCCUPATIONS

In the 18th and 19th centuries, most people in Resolis were working on the land as tenants or agricultural labourers. The usual hierarchy of proprietor or laird, estate manager, tacksman, tenants and mailers is found. Other trades were, of course, represented. In 1792, the following information on trades (and stock) was recorded by the Reverend Robert Arthur:

Millers,	4	Weavers,	27
Ferrymen,	8	Fishermen,	4
Merchant,	1	Dyers,	5
House-carpenters,	8	Coopers,	2
Cartwrights,	2	Corn-mills,	4
Boat-builder,	1	Stills, of 40 gallons each,	3
Blacksmiths,	4	Ferries,	2
Wheel-wrights,	2	Black cattle,	712
Shoemakers,	9	Horses,	356
Tailors, with their		Sheep,	2391
apprentices,	11	Swine, about	30

In 1836, the Reverend Donald Sage recorded that a lint-manufactory, established at Cromarty more than 50 years before, continued to be a great benefit to poor females in Resolis and neighbouring parishes by employing them as spinners and its loss would be very hard upon indigent families.

In Resolis, the same burn powered mills at no less than four locations – Kinbeachie, St Martins, New Mills and Gordon's Mill – the burn changing name from the Kinbeachie Burn to the Newhall Burn to Gordon's Mill Burn from its source to its discharge point in Udale Bay. Additionally, there are records in the 19th century of a complex of mills, including flour and corn, at Poyntzfield powered by water from a tributary of the Newhall Burn. The 1812 and 1844 Braelangwell Estate Plans indicate two different mill complexes, the earlier closer to Braelangwell House, but each fed by water from the Ballicherry Burn before it joins the Newhall Burn.

The precise location of the Miln of Milntown of Rosabrighty or Newhall is not clear, but from 17th and 18th century records it also seems to have been fed by water led from the Ballicherry Burn (water of Carmick) very close to its confluence with the Newhall Burn (water of Gelnie). The same system of a mill dam holding water from the burn which was then fed into the mill waterwheel through a mill lade was generally utilised.

Most of the lands in Resolis were astricted, meaning that tenants were bound to take their grain to a specific mill, paying a toll called multure or thirlage. Sir

William Gordon (died 1742) obtained a Decreet of Adjudication to confirm that certain lands of Newhall, Ardoch (later Poyntzfield), Udol and Braelangwell were strictly thirled to the Mill of Milton of Newhall (*"of old called the Mill of Kintail."*) Despite this, the thirlage was later a source of dispute between Newhall and Poyntzfield Estates.

At the western end of the parish, an 1827 advertisement for a Miller for the Mill of Kinbeachie adds as an incentive *"to which is attached a considerable Thirlage."* Many tenants of the Newhall Estate (even as far east as Alness Ferry) were obliged to have their grain milled at Kinbeachie.

Mills were powered by sources other than water. Horses were commonly used, for example at the small mill at the farmstead to the west of the shore road at Alness Ferry. At Kirkton Farm there was a fixed barn threshing mill, powered firstly by boiler and steam engine. The boiler house chimney still survives, one of few in the Highlands. The chimney is tall to reduce the risk of fire, and is built with hand-made clay bricks, the bond being described as: *"four rows of stretchers, one row of headers, a form of Facing or English Garden-wall Bond."* In the late 19th century, the mill was replaced with one powered by a stationary oil engine. The final engine was last used about 1960 and comprised a 15 horse power electric motor.

There were distilleries in Resolis, both legal and illegal. The legal stills included Braelangwell, said in 1836 to be *"famed for excellent whisky,"* Poyntzfield and, presumably, although there is no direct evidence, at Whiskypark. The illegal stills included one in a bothy at Agneshill which was raided by the Excise in 1850 and one which Hugh Miller implies existed in Castle Craig, but there would have been many more.

Tenants paid their rents in combinations of money or kind (hens, meal, grain). The girnal at Ferryton Point (*"the Storehouse"*) belonged to the Newhall Estate and was where rent in kind was stored by the landlord. Tenants brought their grain or meal to the girnal which had a collecting area at the rear and handed it over to the custodian who acted on the landlord's behalf. The bulky commodity was stored and shipped by sea to the urban markets of the south.

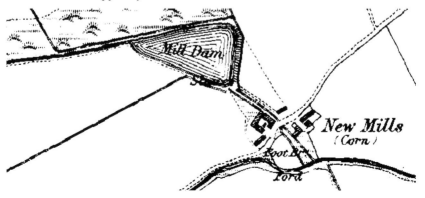

EDUCATION
The Parochial School

In 1616 an act in Privy Council commanded every parish to establish a school *"where convenient means may be had,"* and when the Parliament of Scotland ratified this in 1633 it introduced a tax on local *"heritors"* (landowners) to provide the necessary endowment. However, there were loopholes in this law, and these must have led to the evident difficulties in establishing and maintaining a parish school in Resolis. As appears from the following 1671 document, there were attempts to establish a parish school in 1633 and 1671.

"Ane Act of provisione for the school of Kirkmichell .... Sir Jhon Urquhart .. patron of the united parochs of Kirkmichell and Culicudin, Alexr. Urquhart of Newhall, Jhon Urquhart of Kinbeachie, Mr James Hourston minister of the parochs .... Walter Urquhart in the Ward, Robt. Urqt. in Sant Merteins, Collen Dunbarr in the Birks, Hew Ross in Balcherie wt. divers others of the elders in session ... taking into consideration the great desolatioun for want of ane school ... and that in ... 1633 the ... patron with consent of minister and elders established some competent maintenance for ane qualified schoolmaister ... it was ther will ... that the former act be renewed ... everie dauch in the parish should pay one boll victual ... viz. ... mikle and litle Breyes 1 boll ... Cullicudden 10 firlottis ... Sant Merteins 2 firlottis ... Drumcudden 1 boll ... Kinbeachie 2 fir. ... Craighouse 1 fir. ... Woodhead 1 fir. ... Easter Culbo 2 fir. ... Waster Culbo 1 boll ... Rostabrightie 1 boll ... Davach of the Croft 1 boll ... Breylangwell 1 boll ... Ardach 2 fir. ... Ferritoune and Achmertine 2 fir. ... Waster Belblair 2 fir. ... Easter Belblair 1 fir. ... Risolas 1 fir. ... Bellcherrie 2 fir. all making twall bolls with 3 from patron ... ordered that the school should be erected in some convenient place ... finding that Maister Alexr. Mathow is able and qualified ... do admit and present him."

Despite this, we find in 1718 the Reverend Thomas Inglis lamenting that, despite it being a legal obligation, *"There is no Salarie Setled and modified for maintaining of a Schoolmaster wherethrough the parish is deprived of the benefite of a School to the great hinderance of the Instructing of youth in the principles of the true Reformed Religion."* At this time, the Presbytery agreed *"that the Schoolhouse should be erected in Knocktopeck as the most Centricall place in the parish for that use."* Given that the valued rents of land held by all the heritors in the parish amounted to *"the Summ of Two Thousand Six hundred and Eight pounds Sixteen Shillings Ten pennies Scots Monney; They with the consent and concurrance of the sd Heretors and Parishoners ... appoint the Summ of one Hundred pounds Scots Monney as a Fee & Sallery for a Schoolmaster in the sd parish yearly in all time comeing."* However, in 1721, Mr

Inglis states that they had legal funds designed and appointed for a Schoolmaster but for the present had not a Schoolmaster actually planted.

At long last, in 1777, the Presbytery Records report: *"Thereafter it was represented by Mr Gordon of Newhall and Mr Munro of Poyntzfield, That a schoolhouse had been lately built in the Parish at Newmiln amounting to twelve pound at the public expence, for accommodating the Master and Scholars; and that therefore the said Schoolhouse should be declared to belong to the Parish, and craved, that the Presbytery should so declare: Which Desire the Presbytery found reasonable, and accordingly Declare the said house to be the Parochial Schoolhouse in all time coming."* In 1792, the parochial school was taught by a deserving young man *"who has only £8.6s.8d of stated salary."*

In 1797, the Presbytery considered *"Estimates for building a new Parochial School House at Risolis,"* but concluded the estimates far too expensive and settled for a very simple building. In 1800, the Presbytery took offence that the new parochial schoolmaster, John Munro, had been appointed by the heritors without trial by the Presbytery. The previous teacher, Murdo Cameron, had left the parish. John Munro was not available for interview until he returned from his Session of College at Aberdeen. In 1802, the Presbytery again noted that the recently-appointed parochial Schoolmaster, Mr Thomson, whose school was at New-Miln, had been appointed by the heritors but had not been admitted by the Presbytery as the young man was attending the University of Aberdeen. *"He expects to subsist himself by ye parochial salary, School-Fees & perquisites as Session-Clerk; and will act under the Minister & Presbytery's Direction."* By 1807, a new teacher, Mr Macarthur, had already departed, and Mr Duncan Grant, Student of Philosophy at King's College Aberdeen, was successfully tried in his knowledge in Latin and English, Arithmetic and other Branches commonly taught in parochial schools. In 1812, Duncan was permitted to undertake probationary trials.

By the 1820s, the parochial school is known to be ruinous, and Donald Sage states moreover: *"The parish school of Resolis had at this time a very inefficient teacher..."* Writing about 1824, George Murray, the parish schoolmaster who was to remain in post for an extended period, indignantly states that since his appointment (in 1823) *"and for three years back, the School House and Schoolmaster's apartments have been in a ruinous and uninhabitable state,"* in consequence of which Murray had to utilise part of the manse and then even an old granary at Resolis Farm.

Fortunately, it was rebuilt, as in 1832, the parish school and schoolhouse, occupied by George Murray, is still located at Newmills. Indeed, Sage reports in 1836: *"A very substantial and commodious school-house, with schoolmaster's apartments, has been lately built by the heritors. The present teacher also holds the office of session-clerk. The average number of scholars attending may be about 30. The salary was, in the year 1829, increased from L.16, 17s. 8d. to*

L.30. The school fees scarcely, at an average, amount to L.10 annually."
In due course, it would be replaced by the Education Act school at Newhall in 1876, the Newmills site having acted as the parochial school for 100 years.

Balblair Subscription School

Donald Sage also states that as well as the parish school, in the 1820s, *"there was a little subscription school at Balblair, in the easter end of the parish. This was taught by a young man named Henry Macleod, who kept it in a high state of efficiency and order."*

Drumcudden/Cullicudden School

There had been a long-standing school in Drumcudden, close to the burn to the south of the main road. Presbytery records for 1762 state that the Society for Propagating Christian Knowledge (SPCK) had appointed that the Charity Schoolmaster of Drumcudden Robert Grant be continued at Drumcudden with 11 pounds.

In 1802, the teacher at Drumcudden was George Ross. *"English, Writing, Arithmetic & Bookkeeping. Holds his School daily. Is Supported by the Fees of his Scholars. Acts under the Direction of the Minister of said united parish and has at present Thirty Scholars attending him."*

The Reverend Donald Sage had a dramatic impact on education in Resolis and initiated improvements first in Cullicudden. *"The session felt it to be their duty to furnish the people with the means of education, both secular and religious. At the place of Drumcudden, in the west-end of the parish of Resolis, a school had existed many years previous to my settlement* [in 1822]. *The teacher was Donald Murray, an old man, and the school, like himself, was for years verging into decrepitude. The people, dissatisfied with his mode of teaching, withdrew their children one after another from his school, until the attendance was at last a nullity. The people of the district asked Murray to resign. This he refused to do without some show of reason; for, whilst the people insisted that he should give up the school-buildings, they made no proposals as to where the poor man should go to shelter himself. After discussion, it was ultimately resolved that the school-buildings should be left in Murray's possession, and that new buildings should be erected for the accommodation of a new teacher and the scholars. This arrangement was unanimously agreed to at a meeting held for the purpose; a new site was given and measured out, 200 feet in length and 70 in breadth, sufficient in point of extent, not only for the site of the buildings, but also for a small garden for the schoolmaster. The session undertook to forward the buildings without delay, as well as to collect funds to defray the expenses, all of which was done in the course of three years afterwards* [completed 1826]. *The expenses amounted in all to £48 13s. 1½d., wholly cleared off.*"

The land for the new school had been donated by Thomas McKenzie Paterson Esquire of Drumcudden on perpetual feu.

However, by 1836, Sage reported the school had deteriorated. "*There is another school at Drimcudden, established, in 1823, by the Inverness Education Society. The school-house and schoolmaster's apartments were built by subscription, and by collections made at the church doors, at several different times. The society at Inverness appointed the present teacher, and agreed to pay him a salary of L.19; but afterwards, when their funds were reduced, in consequence of the increased demand for schools, and a number of subscribers having withdrawn, they reduced the schoolmaster's salary from L.19 to L.10. The average number of scholars may be about 20. The fees are very irregularly paid, the greater part of them is paid by equivalents instead of money, that is, by any commodity which the people who are very poor are best able to give. This school at present is in rather an unprosperous state.*"

Even worse, it was subsequently revealed that the new Drumcudden school site had not been legitimately conveyed. The Session Records for 1844 state: "*When the property of Drumcudden was purchased by the late Colin McKenzie Esq*[re.] *of Newhall he found that the late Thomas McKenzie Paterson had no legal right to the property and consequently could not feu any part of it away to the Kirk Session and finding it too near his own private policies built another school at the wester extremity of Drumcudden at his own expense; but did not grant any deed of conveyance to the Kirk Session for the Site and new School-house erected.*"

In the early 1870s, the Ordnance Survey noted, regarding the Cullicudden School at NH649639: "*Free Church School This is a plain substantial building, one storey high, slated and in very good repair. It is supported partly by a committee in Edinburgh, local subscription and school fees. The average attendance is 80, the branches taught are the ordinary branches of English.*"

School heating was by coal fire, and a note from the headteacher of Cullicudden in 1877 is of interest not only in demonstrating the loose funding arrangement but also in its reference to the practice of delivering coal direct to the beach along the Cromarty Firth: "*I have hitherto continued to provide coal and the other attendance required for the use of the School, as I had done for many years back – I always got the year's coal in the Summer Season from Cullicudden beach, when nearest and cheapest; and charged 6d each from all the Scholars who were able and willing to pay. Now, however, there will be additional expense in providing coal and the necessary attendance for the New School, and I wish to lay the whole matter before the School Board."*

These buildings were sold by roup, and the Education Act school at the same location was completed later in 1877.

Sewing School at Cullicudden

In 1792, the Reverend Robert Arthur stated: *"As the bulk of the inhabitants reside towards the extremities of the parish, the parochial school is taught in the east end, and a school for spinning, knitting stockings, and reading English, is established by the Honourable Society, in the wester end, with a salary of 7£."* Sage describes this school as having been a sewing school for young girls, established under the patronage of Mrs Lockhart of Newhall (*i.e.* Henrietta Gordon, died 1799). The female teacher received a salary from the SPCK, it having withdrawn the salary of the Schoolmaster of Drumcudden School.

Jemimaville School

Having sorted out the school for the Cullicudden area, Sage then set about a second school: *"The General Assembly's Schools for the instruction of the children of the poor in the Highlands – having a similar object in view with the Inverness Education Society – were in full operation. As I had already received a school for the west end of the parish from the Inverness Society, I applied to the Assembly's committee for another school in the east end, at Jemimaville. In the month of March, 1826, I received intimation that my claims were favourably entertained."*

In 1836 he states: *"This is one of the Assembly's schools, taught at present by Mr Gilbert M'Culloch, and is certainly one of the most efficient and best taught seminaries in the north. The intellectual system has been adopted, and with great success. Many young men taught at this school are now the teachers of subscription schools through the country, very much to the satisfaction of their employers."* The school and schoolmaster's house here were paid for solely by Major Munro of Poyntzfield. After the Disruption of 1843, this became a Free Church school. In 1958, this building, near the old Free Church, was in use as a store. It became the home of Jane Duncan, who died there in 1976.

Education Act Schools at Newhall and Cullicudden

Following the Education (Scotland) Act 1872, which made compulsory for the first time education of all children from 5 to 13, two new schools were constructed, one replacing the existing school on the Cullicudden site, opening to pupils in 1877, and another built on a fresh Newhall site, opening to pupils in 1876, these continuing as the sole Resolis schools for 130 years. The architect of both the schools and associated schoolhouses was Alexander Ross of Inverness and he organised the contractors and tradesmen.

The Cullicudden opening was celebrated in the press. It had been eagerly awaited – the headteacher in 1877 reported: "*The Scholars are longing to be admitted to the New School. The bad ventilation in the old school, with the bad kind of desks & seats are unfavourable to the health and progress of the School, especially in the Summer Season. Very few new Scholars have entered at this time: They seem to be waiting for the opening of the new School.*" To add icing to the cake, at the opening ceremony "*Mrs Shaw Mackenzie, of Newhall, kindly ordered 20s worth of confections to be distributed among the delighted pupils.*"

The building of the two Education Act schools at Newhall and Cullicudden

Cullicudden Primary School; opened 1877; closed as a school 2007.

had in fact been fraught with delays and works not being to specification. The School Board was resolute with Alexander Ross, not authorising payment of contractors until all work was completed to their satisfaction. In the case of Newhall, which opened to pupils the previous year, some building works were still going on when the pupils were in place. The rigour of the Board resulted in buildings which admirably performed their function for 130 years.

School Board records and school log books of the 19th and early 20th century show that attendance dipped considerably during harvest and other times of agricultural need or when poor weather or infectious disease occurred. An unpopular headmaster at one school would lead to some pupils being enrolled at the other. A truancy officer (known as *"the Whipper-In"* when Mr Matheson Bog of Cullicudden was in post) was employed, but was resented by some parents who needed their children's assistance with farmwork. The only education most children received was provided by these schools – they left at 14 to work full time, unless they were the exceptional pupils to go on to an Academy, perhaps on a bursary.

Shelters in each schoolyard were built in 1909 and soup kitchens instituted in 1911. The Board resolved in 1912 to provide *"during the winter months coffee and cocoa & milk instead of the usual soup."* A Cullicudden photograph (see

Newhall Primary School; opened 1876; closed as a school 2007.

back cover) shows an unidentified schoolmaster and Miss Annie Violet Kemp, assistant teacher, in the yard *c*1914 pouring cocoa for the children. School photographs of the 1920s show that even then children were commonly attending school barefoot in summer.

The new schools were regularly used for concerts, dances, meetings and even *"cinematographic entertainments."* Parish tradition refers to Prince, Mr Black of Newhall's dog, as an ill-tempered animal, and, indeed, the Board in 1908 ordered Mr Black, following complaints (including one involving a child too frightened to attend school after being bitten) to confine his dog during school hours. But the strangest event was a saga 1912-1914 at Newhall regarding tracing who should be responsible for removal of a 68 pound artillery gun "*a source of danger & annoyance*" which had been allowed to be used for practice by the Artillery Volunteers in the schoolyard!

Discipline was very strict but there are few complaints in the Board records. In 1877, the Newhall schoolmaster was being pursued by a small number of parents (such pursuits sadly still common in country schools), one of the issues in his case being excessive punishment. His response was not contrite: "As *to the flogging I deny that ever any child was any worse of any punishment I gave but a good deal the better, and I deny that I ever used my fists.*"

School gardens were established to teach agricultural principles – H.M. Inspectors' instructions in 1917 to Cullicudden were: "3 *lessons per week of one hour each in summer, and 2 lessons of one hour each for the rest of the year – Extra time to be entered in the Log Book.*" Newhall has some charming pictures of boys at work in the garden, following their winning the County prize in 1922.

Schoolmasters were assisted by monitors, pupils who stayed on to assist, but their payment was by no means assured. In 1877, the Newhall headmaster writes to the Board: "*Allow me to remind you that the two monitors who were assisting me during last year … are still unpaid for their services.*"

Again, in 1879, former monitor Mina Noble writes to the headteacher: "*I was told that you had said there was £10 lost on my account and Taylor says 'I have deprived the school of a large sum' You all speak as if I had swindled you out of it. I do think it is rather cowardly of so many learned men trying to take the advantage of a young girl like me. I am under the impression it has been done all along. If any money has been lost on my account I should think it would be with not having me under an engagement. But that is not my fault. The School Board neglected to do that. I should like everything explained. If you would be so good as write and do so. I had no idea you would have 'turned the tables' on me like that. I always thought you were so kind & considerate. But perhaps you have caught the infection since you came to Resolis, of the Resolis folks' ways.*" However, the headteacher, Mr Morgan, set the matter right.

Some headteachers were not averse to publicity, and the Reverend Robert McDougall attacked the practice in 1879 following a newspaper article extolling the virtues of the education and recent examination event at Newhall Primary – whether or not the vitriol was heated by the leading role in the event of the rival minister in the parish can only be conjectured: "*There is little doubt but the wretched & untrue puff was sent to the papers by Mr. Morgan himself who by the way presumes to speak for the school from its opening day. Under these circumstances you see the necessity, in the interests of truth, of having the Government Inspector's Reports published to prevent undue inflation of Windbags.*"

In latter years, Government Inspectors' Reports were indeed to note the schools as providing an excellent standard of education.

Resolis Primary School

With pupil rolls falling, there was pressure in the 1990s and 2000s to close at least one of Cullicudden and Newhall Primary Schools. Following a decision to amalgamate the two schools through a Public Private Partnership programme of new school provision, both Newhall and Cullicudden closed in 2007.

The new Resolis Primary School, with its modern educational facilities, at the south east corner of the Resolis Crossroads, opened for use on 18 April 2007. The opening was marked by a symbolic march of the pupils of the two old schools, together, to the sound of the pipes, up the Church Brae and through the doorway of the new school.

The formal opening took place nearly a year later, on 25 January 2008. Mrs Essie Munro, once a pupil at Newhall, and formerly a cook at Cullicudden, and a long-time resident of Resolis (dwelling in Alness Ferry for many years), was guest of honour.

The new school provides a nursery and other community functions. The school badge design by Alison Bisset was chosen by competition. It consists of a sun rising over a sloping field to allude to "*Slope of Light, or Resolis*," the field striped brown and green to reflect arable and grass agricultural traditions, over a blue sea to symbolise the Firth and its historical importance to Resolis.

Resolis Primary School; opened 2007.

ORGANISED RELIGION

Early references to the two parishes of Kirkmichael and Cullicudden in Roman Catholic days are mainly from Vatican records of disputes referred to the Pope for resolution. Kirkmichael features much more frequently than Cullicudden.

Parish of Cullicudden

The first reference to Cullicudden as a parish is in the year 1227. Jeronimus the parson of Culicuden is a signatory at Kenedor in Moray at the settlement of a dispute between the bishops of Moray and of Ross about the churches of Kyntalargyn and Ardrosser: "... *Ego Willelmus Poer persona de Lemnelar . Ego Jeronimus persona de Culicuden . Ego Thomas persona de Sudy ...*"

Parish teinds as initially introduced belonged to the incumbent (parson or rector) of the parish. However, most were granted to a corporation or an individual, who took over the rectorial rights, with the remainder consequently going to a poorly-paid substitute known as the vicar who actually ministered in the parish. This weakening of the parish to the benefit of other religious institutions is recognised as being a major factor in the decline of the medieval church in Scotland.

The parsonage of Cullicudden was apparently one of the prebends (shared revenues) of the cathedral of Ross erected c1255/6, and although no definite proof of this exists until 1378, both parsonage and vicarage appear in Bagimond (a late 13th century taxation roll) as separate assessments, as they continue to do after certain proof of the prebend's continuance is available.

On 5 October 1440 David Stewart MA, clerk, diocese of St Andrews, son of

Cullicudden Church, south aisle. The door lintel bears the date 1609.

the earl of Mar and kinsman of James king of Scots, supplicates the Pope to provide him to the vacant archdeaconry of Caithness, notwithstanding his holding the canonry and prebend of Culecadin in the church of Ross (£8).

At the Reformation (1560) the parson of Cullicudden was David Dunbar. In 1574 William Monro Hucheson was the reader. In 1580 (14 October) King James VI presented Master George Thomsoun to the parsonage of Killecuddin, vacant by the decease of Master David Dunbar but strangely in the same year (1 December) he presented William Monro Hucheonsoun to the same parsonage, vacant by decease of the same Master David. As Thomsoun and Hucheonson were each to be examined and admitted if found qualified to serve as a minister, presumably Thomsoun failed or was disqualified for some other reason.

The Reverend Robert Arthur suggested in 1792 that Resolis "*had formerly been divided into three, Kirkmichael, Cullicudden and St. Martin's, as appears not only from old charters and tradition, but from the burial grounds and remains of the old churches still visible in each of them.*" The Reverend Donald Sage (1836), in contrast, suggested: "*It is probable, however, that St Martin's, or Kirk Martin, and not Cullicudden, was the name originally of this small but ancient parish. It is still called by the natives* Sgire' a' Mhartinn, *or the parish of St Martin's; and at the place of St Martin's, a small farm near its western extremity, the foundations of a church, surrounded by a burying-ground not now occupied, may still be seen. The probability is, therefore, that the parish church, dedicated to St Martin of Tours, was originally at the place of St Martin's; but the church being afterwards removed to the more centrical place of Cullicudden, the parish from this circumstance came to be so called.*"

In fact, there is a frustrating lack of hard information on the background to the church at St Martins (see St Martins) and there is no strong evidence to support either of these theories.

Site of St Martins Church, below Drumdyre.

Parish of Kirkmichael

For a detailed appraisal of the Kirk and Parish of Kirkmichael, see "*Kirkmichael, A Short History.*" This parish, united to Cullicudden in 1662, forms the eastern portion of the united parish. It is not yet known when Kirkmichael as a parish was created. Parish division in this area occurred about the time of the organisation of the Bishopric of Ross *c*1128 but absence of early references could mean that Kirkmichael was a later creation. The parsonage of Kirkmichael had been erected into a prebend of Ross by 1429 (the date of the first document to mention Kirkmichael) and so continued, the cure being a vicarage perpetual.

For some time before and after 1429, possession of the canon and prebend of Kirkmichael formed the subject of intense competition between many clerics, none of whom probably ever set foot in the parish. Later Kirkmichael clergy can also be identified from documents of their time. For example, a 1533 charter is witnessed by Master John Innes, rector of Kirkmichell. In 1547, Queen Mary presented Robert Marioribanks to the prebend of Kirkmichael in the cathedral church of Ross, vacant by the decease of Master John Innes. In 1548, she presented Thomas Marioribankis, the son of Master Thomas Marioribankis burgess of Edinburgh, to the same prebend, vacant by the decease of Robert Marioribankis. He is presented on the same date to other benefices elsewhere in Scotland, demonstrating the tenuous connection of prebends with the actual parish.

In 1570 and 1574 Alexander Clunes was reader at Kirkmichael. In 1580, 1585 and 1586 the rector of Kirkmichell was Master Thomas Marioribanks. In 1587 King James VI presented Alexander Reid to the vicarage of Kirkmichael, vacant by the decease of Sir James Gray.

Kirkmichael, from a photograph *c*1906 held by Mrs Essie Munro.
From L to R: the now-demolished west gable with belfry, under which Hugh
Miller worked, the Gun Munro mausoleum, and the east gable.

The *"Centrical"* Church

When the two parishes of Kirkmichael (the eastern part of Resolis) and Cullicudden (the western part of Resolis) were united by Act of Parliament in 1662, a new *"centrical"* church was commanded to be built at Resolis, near the centre of the unified parish.

Although it was a long time before the new church was built, the unification of the two parishes in 1662 meant that there was a surplus church, manse, glebe and post of minister.

The minister issue was straightforward, as it appears in 1662 the Cullicudden post was vacant, whilst James Houston (son of John Houston the Wardlaw minister) seems to have been appointed to Kirkmichael before the two parishes were united. In 1684 he granted, with the Bishop's consent, a tack of the teinds of Drumcudden to William Duff, a baillie of Inverness. He remained in office until he died in 1714, apparently never having conformed to Presbyterianism. On his death, the Presbytery was able to install the obviously highly-regarded Thomas Inglis (he was ordained at Kirkmichael on 26 May 1715). Curiously, despite Houston never being admitted to the Presbytery, he could not have been actively opposed to the new Established Church, as the Presbytery of Chanonry met frequently in the early 1700s in the parish at Kirkmichael, Cullicudden or houses in the parish such as *"Ballacherie."*

Despite the 1662 command for a new centrical church, the two existing churches continued to be used in increasingly dilapidated condition and it was 1769 before the new church was completed, following eventual agreement with the estate proprietors who paid for it pro rata according to their estate within the parish.

Resolis Church, completed 1769. Scene of the 1843 Resolis Riot.
Sold by the Church of Scotland 2005 and now subject of a residential conversion.

The precise location of the original two manses is not known but would have been close to the original churches. Initially it appears that the minister continued to use the Kirkmichael manse, which fell into such dereliction that there was agreement for it to be completely rebuilt in 1716 for Mr Thomas Inglis, "*that in order to build a competent Manse for the Minister, the said dwelling house must be throwen down to the foundation.*" At some time thereafter, a new manse was built for the minister at the more central location of Resolis. This manse itself was not ideal and seemed to need constant repair or improvement and was eventually rebuilt to the minister's satisfaction.

The new manse meant that the minister's two Glebes were distant. When the new church was being built in 1769, William Gordon of Newhall (who held the patronage of the parish) was asked if he was willing to give a Piece of his Lands in Exchange for the "*present two Glebes the one lying at Cullicudden and the other at Kirkmichael and each of them surrounded on all sides by Mr Gordon's Lands. To which Mr Gordon replied that he was willing to accept of Mr McPhail's two Glebes & to give for them an Equivalent of his Land out of the Tack of Risollis as lying most adjacent to the present manse in order thereby to accommodate Mr McPhail the present Incumbent & his Successors in office.*" The Reverend Robert Arthur was later to be critical: "*The glebe consisted, at the incumbent's admission* [1774]*, of 19 acres of poor moorish soil arable, and about 12 acres of barren stoney moor.*"

Of the two original churches of Kirkmichael and Cullicudden, much of Kirkmichael remains, although only portions of the medieval church are retained within the structure, whilst merely short lengths of walls, with a datestone of 1609, remain standing at Cullicudden.

The Free Churches

In the Disruption of 1843, most of the Resolis parishioners "*came out*" with the Reverend Donald Sage to join the new Free Church. The violent resistance by several hundred parishioners to the induction of the replacement Established Church minister at Resolis, the capture of one of the female parishioners and her rescue from the Cromarty Gaol, are all described within the Alston booklet.

Following the Disruption, the Free Church congregation initially met on 19 June 1843 at "*John Holm's Croft, Resolis*" where, following prayer, it was revealed that whilst the Newhall Proprietor would not grant them a site for a new church, Sir George Munro of Poyntzfield was most willing to grant a site at Jemimaville. "*This offer was, notwithstanding the obvious inconvenience of the locality to the great majority of the people, and after considerable discussion,*" *finally accepted."* The walls of the first Resolis Free Church, close to the shore, are still standing.

A note *"At the Storehouse of Newhall, Nov.ʳ 1843"* states that Newhall having kindly granted to the Free Church congregation the use of the Storehouse, *"until their own church now in course of erection should be finished, a large number of the male heads of families and others met here this day for the purpose of fitting up the Storehouse for the stated assembling of the congregation."* Services took place in the upper floor but, the storehouse being dark and relatively small, were carried on outside when weather permitted.

The original Free Church in Resolis, Jemimaville.

The new Free Church from the outset was not suited to much of the parish, and eventually a more central site at the present location was obtained and the new church built there, in 1867. Sage moved from the original Free Church manse (see Jemimaville) to a handsome new manse built close to the new church.

The present Free Church, constructed 1867.

Other Church Buildings in Resolis

Nationally, some members of the Free Church joined with the United Presbyterian Church in 1900 to form the United Free Church. A United Free Church building was erected at Newmills in 1906 (later re-erected as Scott's garage in Jemimaville, just outside the parish). The manse was the house now known as Ellenslea at the lower entrance to Braelangwell.

Scott's Garage,
Jemimaville.

Finally, the former Church of Scotland Mission Hall, which was used as a Public Hall for a long time, stands disused at the west end of Jemimaville.

Former Church of
Scotland Mission Hall,
Jemimaville.

The Present Day

At time of writing, the only functioning church building in Resolis is the Free Church; one of the three locations where the Minister of "*Ferintosh and Resolis Free Church*" preaches weekly.

Adherents of the Church of Scotland travel to Findon Hall Culbokie, where the minister of the Resolis and Urquhart Church of Scotland preaches. In this context, the modern parish has been "*the United Parish of Resolis and Urquhart*" since 1961.

LAW AND DISORDER

Legal proceedings, both criminal and civil, involving people or land in Resolis are a rich source of historical and social information. Within even the dry and complex legal cases arising from inheritance issues (and there are many examples associated with Resolis estates) little nuggets of interest can be found, while a good murder can present a window into the past. The following examples are principally drawn from dusty National Archive records.

Murder

The murder of Captain George Munro (living at Chapelton) by Robert Ferguson in 1812, the culmination of a neighbour dispute, and leading to Ferguson's public hanging, is the most notable historical Resolis murder. The case attracted considerable attention at the time, the tragedy soon after being made the subject of a mournful half-English half-Gaelic ballad. Details of the incident can be found in my article in the bibliography.

Munro, a powerful and handsome man, and a great swordsman, came into the Smiddy at Kirktown and began berating and beating Ferguson, a boatbuilder, for complaining to Captain MacKenzie of Newhall, the Proprietor. There had been a dispute the preceding day between Captain Munro and Ferguson's wife regarding the privilege of pasturing Ferguson's cow on the meadow grass near the Shore or Ferry Side. Captain Munro expressed himself thus, "*Damn you and Captain MacKenzie,*" and struck Ferguson violently several times.

Ferguson, who had been drinking in the Balblair Inn earlier, deployed a knife he used in his trade, whereupon Captain Munro exclaimed, "*The Scoundrell has wounded me and brought out my Guts.*" Ferguson was brought to Newhall House, but, while the Proprietor was being informed, Ferguson returned homewards, took the Small boat of the Ferry, and absconded to the North Side. He proceeded to a house in Saltburn where he drank a bottle of beer; it was there that he was apprehended by a Party of Constables on a Warrant from Captain MacKenzie.

Munro died the following day, lamenting, "*would he had fallen in the field of battle.*" At the subsequent Circuit Court trial at Inverness, Ferguson's plea of self-defence was not sustained, and he was condemned to be hung and his body given over for public dissection.

Whilst in prison, Ferguson learned to read and was converted to God. At the place of execution, on the Commons at Inverness, he addressed the surrounding multitude in Gaelic at length. "*After his exhortation he mounted the drop without the least trepidation, and, after delivering a most impressive prayer, he was launched into eternity without a struggle. Throughout the whole of this awful scene the unfortunate man displayed the most heroic firmness and Christian resignation, and spoke with a clearness and consistency that astonished all who heard him."*

Riots

Details of the Agneshill whisky still affair are provided in the Gazetteer, and for details of the 1843 religious Resolis Riot and subsequent jail-break at Cromarty, see the well-researched booklet by Alston available from Cromarty Courthouse.

There were other riots in the area. For example, the food shortages of 1847 led to rioting in many locations across Scotland, including around the shoreside girnals and piers of the Moray Firth where grain was being exported while local people starved. The following extract from a letter, dated 5 March 1847, from the Procurator Fiscal in Cromarty to the Crown Agent in Edinburgh, gives a picture of the times but also provides information on the Cullicudden Quarry:

"Sir, I have to report that a Steam Boat belonging to Donald Urquhart Quarrier at Culliculden in the Parish of Resolis, having on the afternoon of the 4th. current arrived at the Beach, near the Harbour of Cromarty for the purpose of discharging a Cargo of Stones, a number of riotous and evil disposed persons assembled and violently attacked the Boat. The Rioters then tore away some of the Sails, Ropes, Blocks, and the Rudder of the Boat. The mob afterwards took possession of a small Boat belonging to Urquhart which he uses for carrying himself and his crew from the Steam boat to the shore and dragged it furiously through the streets of the Town in a riotous and disorderly manner. The more peaceable portion of the inhabitants being afraid to interfere with them. On enquiring I am informed that this attack and riot arose out of the Circumstances of Urquhart having sometime before in the exercise of his Calling as a Boatman Conveyed a small quantity of Grain from the shore below Finden in the Parish of Urquhart to a ship at that time lying in the Roads of Cromarty."

Three Urquhart brothers, quarriers in Cullicudden, had actually been involved in the 1843 religious riot themselves.

Theft and Poaching

The usual minor thefts occurred, involving money, implements, timber, clothes – anything that proved to be too tempting. Particularly common was poaching game from the estate moors, or stealing saplings or timber for fire.

For example, in 1847, a Mr Ure, woodmerchant, Maryburgh had purchased standing wood at Newhall for use as sleepers and barrel staves. William Fraser and John Fraser, sawyers, Agnes Hill, had cut the wood and left it on the beach. However, the wood was removed overnight. Witnesses saw Nelly Holm, Janet Ross and Margaret Fraser, all Balblair, remove the wood. Nelly Holm and others accepted taking some wood as fuel.

The following amusiong newspaper article from 4 March 1836 describes a theft leading to the search of the entire village of Jemimaville – except for the house of the only person above suspicion, the schoolmaster!

"THEFT.– As Finlay Macrae, Millar at Poyntzfield, was returning from Cromarty, on Saturday last, he repaired with a few friends to the Inn at Jemima Village, leaving his cart, containing a barrel of herring, some loaf bread, and a quantity of fresh fish, &c., standing at the door. On coming out of the Inn, he was not a little surprised to find that the whole of the articles in his cart, with the exception of the herring, had disappeared. He instantly procured a Warrant from a Justice of the Peace in the immediate neighbourhood, and caused an active Constable, resident on the spot, to search the whole of the houses in the Village, with the exception of the Schoolmasters; no traces, however, of the stolen articles could be discovered, and the thief continued in the possession of the loaves and fishes.– Alas! poor Finlay!"

Assault

Assaults were surprisingly common in Resolis in the 19th century; many of them occurred in or close to the Inns so that it can be safely assumed that alcohol was often a contributing factor. The Court records show an astonishing number of assaults (and breaches of the peace, thefts and road offences) associated with two families of hawkers or tinkers at Jemimaville named MacPhee and Williamson, with cases in 1897, 1900, 1910, 1914, 1915, 1917 and 1926.

Inquiries into Fatal Accidents

There are several sad cases of inquiries into fatal accidents, often involving agricultural labourers. For example, in 1896, labourer John Ross died after being caught by the revolving drum of a portable steam threshing mill at Sheep Park.

High Jinks

There were cases of high jinks that went wrong. One of the most serious occurred in 1843, when John McLennan, farm servant of John Nicol at Culbo, was charged with carrying out a mischievous act that resulted in serious injury.

At a wedding dance, he had placed gunpowder in the pipe of John Shaw, a lad of weak intellect, and induced him to smoke it. The pipe exploded when lit, causing burning, injury and the loss of sight in one eye.

War Offences

All sorts of offences occurred, wittingly or unwittingly, due to the proliferation of regulations during the First World War.

In 1915, William Macpherson, Springfield, was fined £2 for displaying light visible from outside during black-out hours. Also in 1915, Alexander Macdonald, Cullicudden, was fined 10s for displaying a light between sunset and sunrise, visible from the Cromarty Firth. In 1917, Catherine Thom, Jemimaville, was fined 10s for the same offence.

In 1917, Captain James Pelham Burn, 3rd Battalion Seaforth Highlanders, was fined £27 for contravening the Motor Spirit Contravention Order by using petrol to drive a car from Cromarty to Braelangwell Lodge for the purpose of shooting game on Braelangwell Moor.

The most serious offence in this context involved William MacPhee, Hawker, Jemimaville, who in 1918 was given 60 days with hard labour for concealing a deserter, Private Andrew MacPhee.

Debt

Several hundreds of cases are recorded relating to debt within Resolis. These range from minor cases of non-payment for services or goods to significant debts leading to bankruptcy of businesses or removal of tenants.

To give an example of the kinds of people and sums involved, the following information appears in an 1838 Summons of Arrears raised by Colin MacKenzie Esquire of Newhall, which resulted in the Sheriff Officers summoning and charging seven of his tenants with arrears of rent. These were:

"Angus Fraser Tenant in Brae the sum of Fifteen Pounds thirteen Shillings Sterling being the Am of arrears of rent and road Money due by him to the Pursuer for Lands possessed by him in Brae at and preceeding the term of Martinmas last*

William Cameron Tenant in Sheep-Park £8.3.2

Alexander MacKenzie Ferryman Balblair £2.0.0

Margaret Fraser or Ferguson – Widow of the late Donald Ferguson Ferryman at Balblair £4.19.6

William Holm Church Officer Risolis £5.10.0

John Urquhart Pensioner in Agneshill £4.11.2"

Three were able to make partial payment and the claim was reduced in consequence, but all were decerned against for the claims made, and for expenses of process.

Removal of Tenants

There are copious civil cases involving the removal of estate tenants who had fallen behind in their payments to all of the Resolis estates. In times of hardship, there could be many of these in a single year. In the 1830s, at the instigation of Colin Mackenzie of Newhall, several dozen tenants were removed.

It has been suggested that some of these particular removals were to allow longer term and more enlightened tenancies to be established. Certainly observers in the 18th and 19th centuries bemoaned the tenancy system at the time as being too short term and wrongly structured, giving tenants no incentive to improve land or buildings. Robert Arthur, in 1792, said: "*With only one exception, a lease was never given in this parish for a longer period than 7 years, till, in the year 1782, the late Mr. George Munro gave leases to 2 tenants for 19 and 21 years: Since that time, many leases have been given on the estate of Newhall for 21 years, besides melioration for enclosing the farms, and bringing moor into arable land.*"

The Election Dispute

One of the longest and most complex Scottish legal disputes of the 18th century revolved around land in Resolis. Sir John Gordon of Invergordon wished to become Member of Parliament for Cromarty-shire in opposition to Mr William Pulteney. In 1765 he set about the establishment of voters in the County who would later support him at election. At this time, a voter had to be at least a freeholder in the County, and hence Sir John transferred the freehold in numerous areas of land to friends and relations, hastening the process of recording the transfers in the sasine records, whilst retaining the interest in Meikle and Little Braes to allow himself to continue to qualify.

The existing Freeholders subsequently refused to admit these claimants to the Roll of Freeholders in the County, on grounds including that the sasines had not been properly registered for the required full year. Moreover, they challenged Sir John's own remaining qualification through the lands of Brae, and, through various stratagems, the qualifications of his nephew, William Gordon of Newhall. The resulting legal dispute amounts to a hefty volume of material, in which, usefully, there is minute inspection of and deliberation over old charters and retours, many involving land in Resolis.

The Mulbuie Commonty Case

The break-up of the Mulbuie Commonty amongst the Black Isle estates was preceded by lengthy legal proceedings and several abortive attempts to divide the land legally, and illegally. Even that most proprietor-sympathetic of ministers, Robert Arthur, in 1810 appealed to the Presbytery to take action against David Urquhart of Braelangwell and Donald Mackenzie of Newhall.

In Arthur's words, Urquhart *"had settled a number of Mealers or Cotters on the nearest and best part of the Common called the Mulbuy, to the south side of the Burn called Aultdouack, and had, with Mackenzie, carried out very extensive fir plantations on the Common thereby preventing the obtaining of pasturage and fuel, and had shut up two Public Roads, the one from the Ferry of Alness, to Fortrose, & Ferry of Fort-George; and which was always the Kirk-Road from the wester end of the Estate of Poyntzfield, & part of the Estate of Brealangwell. The other Road leading from the Manse of Risolis to said Common & Inverness; by which a great number of parishioners to the North & East of the Manse, brought their Fuel from the Mulbuy; & which was also a common Road to the Church. In consequence of the shutting of the first, all Travellers from the Ferry of Alness to Fortrose & the Ferry of Fort-George, have to ride, or walk, a Mile more than formerly: as has your petitioner, when going to the Presbytery Seat."* The Presbytery referred the matter to the Assembly which promised action when it could afford it.

Evidence in 1816 was heard from many Resolis parishioners who used the moors for grazing stock or obtaining fuel or roofing material. They lost the use of this resource when the Court of Session in 1827 finally allocated the Commonty to the different estates. In Resolis, only Urquhart of Kinbeachy had the conscience to give some compensation (£2 per annum) to the poor.

The evidence given in 1816 by dozens of Black Isle tenants represents a valuable source of information, particularly when read with the detailed map drawn up for the case.

"John Mackenzie, mailer on the lands of Easter Raddery, aged 66, born at Poyntzfield, resided in the neighbourhood of the Whitebog for forty-two years ... recollects putting up his own house thirty-seven years ago on the Whitebog, and he remembers at the time having some disputes with the tenants of Cromarty; in consequence of which, he went to Mr Rose, then factor on the estate of Cromarty, who told him that he might go with his plough till his ox struck his horn in Poyntzfield's dike. Depones ... the present road to Inverbreaky Ferry was made forty-three years ago, and the deponent assisted in making it."

"William Holm, proofsman on the estate of Newhall, residing at Ferrytown, aged 72 ... remembers all the different proprietors of the estate of Newhall for more than 60 years; and he knows all the farms upon the said estate; and that

the tenants of these farms, and the ferriers at Inverbreaky, uniformly all and
every of them frequented the commonties of Milbuy, Brae, and Cromarty, some
by pasturing their cattle, and others by cutting turf and divot, and never were
interrupted."

"John Maclean ... has resided on the estate of Brae all his life, as did his
predecessors for some generations, and is well acquainted with the boundary of
the claimant's estate to the south: That the march commences at the south-east,
at the corner of Mr Munro of Poyntzfield's Wood of Brae, where a march-stone
was placed by the late Mr Urquhart: That the boundary at the south-west is a
dike dividing the claimant's estate from the estate of Easter Culbo: That the
deponent is not acquainted with the precise line running from the one point to
the other, but that the Fleucheries is a good way to the north of the line he has
described. Being interrogated ... When the crofts and houses at Agnes Hill were
first placed? depones, That it was about thirty years and more, but not forty, and
as he believes by the late Mr Urquhart. What was the occupation of the ground
at Agnes Hill before the crofts and houses were placed there? depones, That it
was used for pasture by the tenants of Brae for their cattle, and he has seen Mr
Barclay's cattle from Kirktown of Newhall there, when Mr Barclay was
tacksman, but never saw the cattle from any other estate there."

The high ground in Resolis
has been in use by man for
thousands of years.

Above: Long Cairn above
Wester Brae (see pages 9, 67).

Left: Chambered Cairn above
Woodhead (see pages 9, 129).

MORAL POLICING
The Kirk Session and the Presbytery

The Kirk Session Records for Resolis commence only in 1822, earlier records sadly having been destroyed by the Reverend Robert Arthur, so the picture of moral policing and church business found in other parishes is incomplete for Resolis. Fortunately, the more serious cases were reported upwards to the Presbytery, in whose records some early Resolis cases can be found.

The Kirk Session went to particular lengths to find out paternity in cases of illegitimacy. There were financial as well as moral reasons for this, for if the father of an illegitimate child could be identified then he could be charged with its maintenance. Nevertheless the zeal with which such investigations were prosecuted makes uncomfortable reading in this more tolerant age. Some examples are provided.

The earliest Resolis case in the records relates to William McCulloch in Ardoch and Isobel Mckenzie in Udale, who were accused of a long standing illicit relationship. William had been banned from associating with Isobel and in 1705 had been appointed to purge himself by Oath before the Congregation but did not, with fresh Scandal being reported to the Presbytery. William was threatened with excommunication if he did not "*confess his sin of Incest & adultery wherewith he was charged. To which he answered, That it would be a sin to confess that whereof he was not guilty.*" Eventually, following advice from the Synod and Assembly, William and Isobel were excommunicated in 1710: "*Therefore the presbitry did & hereby do Excommunicate the said William McCulloch & Isobel Mckenzie In the name of the Lord Jesus Christ, the allone King & head of His Church, and deliver them over to Satan, for the destruction of the flesh, that the Spirit may be saved in the day of the Lord. They being in This was intimate to them, & appointed to be read, at the most patent Church door.*"

A more typical incident would be as in this 1721 report: "*A Reference was given in from the Session of Cullecudon – bearing that Donald Mccay a married person having Confessed his being guilty of Adultery with Jean Urquhart daughter to Thomas Urquhart in Knocktopack an unmarried woman. The Session did refer him to the presbytery and cited him apud acta to this dyet, And the said Donald Mccay being call'd compeared, and being Interrogat he adhered to his former confession before the Session, and being spoken to concerning the haynousness of his sin was referred back to the Session satisfy according to discipline.*"

In an unusual case in 1828, Margaret Robertson living at Resolis and Robert McLeod a saddler at Invergordon, were delated for fornication. McLeod protested that the real father was James Bayne at Invergordon, and produced a document signed by Bayne confessing the same. However, investigation showed that McLeod himself had tried to get the lady to drink a phial of Muriatic acid to procure an abortion, the phial of which was retained by the Session. It further became apparent that McLeod had bribed Bayne with the offer of half a guinea to sign the false confession.

Other sins brought before the Session and Presbytery included Sabbath Profanation (such as sailing a boat for pleasure, drinking whisky and gathering ware), sexual offences and charming, examples of which are given within the Gazetteer. The common penalty was to be appointed to stand before the congregation to be publicly rebuked for three Sabbaths successively, a punishment not accepted by all.

The Pulpit (now removed) in the Church of Scotland,
from which the minister would rebuke sinners.

The strongest opposition in Resolis to the whole process came in 1836 from George Gordon Smith, Surgeon in Cromarty, who admitted fornication with Margaret McNear alias Widow Munro in Agness Hill. *"George G. Smith was then interrogated, if on the ground of his confession he was willing to submit to the discipline of the Church & to which he replied that he did not consider any discipline necessary in the case, as it was his opinion that all external forms of Repentance were merely popish, that he would however, be willing to submit to a private admonition from the Session & be absolved. Being told that the Scriptures enforced rebuking* 'them that sin before all,' *the passage 1 Timothy 6.20 being read to him, he replied that he considered that passage as popish also & that it should be expunged from the Scriptures like as other parts of the Scriptures, called the Apocrypha have already been, on account of their popish errors. Being seriously dealt with in regard to his impenitency for his offence as well as for his infidel sentiments, he replied that he did not come here today for the purpose of hearing such sort of homilies, and then went away."*

Defamation

The Resolis Kirk Session also investigated cases of defamation of character.

In 1824, Lillias Urquhart in Bog of Cullicudden, a communicant, complained that Jean McLean and Jean Simpson had been spreading a story that she, when in the service of one Murray, had stolen some whisky. The Session, having investigated, recorded in the minute her innocence of the false and malicious charges.

In a case in 1833, which involved evidence from a considerable number of parishioners, and deplorable behaviour from all concerned, Mary McRea, wife of Alexander Munro, was found guilty of defamation of character of Thomas and Anne Munro, all residing at Culbo, and Thomas and Anne were cleared of the accusations against them.

The most extreme case was in 1834, when the whole parish was awash with rumours of a romantic liaison between the wife of the Poyntzfield grieve and a Captain Mackenzie, a guest of the Laird of Poyntzfield, Major George Gun Munro. The Session's investigation involved interviewing many of the Poyntzfield servants and other parishioners, including Alexander Urquhart, the Dancing Master in Jemimaville, who was suspected by Captain Mackenzie as the author of anonymous letters implicating the pair. Extraordinary scenes were reported.

Major Munro stated that one morning *"he and his family whilst at Breakfast were thrown into great agitation by seeing his friend Captain Mackinzie coming on the lawn before his house apparently lame & supported by Alexander Urquhart Dancing Master at Jamima Ville & by Witness' Brother Mr Robert*

Munro." The reason? When Urquhart was asked by Captain Mackenzie to be examined by Major Munro under oath, *"he said he was willing to go, but that he must be allowed first to go home & wash his face that Capt Mackinzie put his stick out before him & said with an oath that he should not go home but come up with him directly. Declares that he sprung over a fence to get off from Capt Mackinzie and that Capt Mackinzie pursued him & sprung over a ditch struck him with a stick in his hand & broke it with the violence of the blow on his shoulder. Declares that in springing over the ditch in pursuit of him Capt Mackinzie sprained his foot but had a hold of him & lay upon him as he was lying down upon the ground."*

The case had many other elements of a farce. A key issue was what had occurred when Captain Mackenzie and the grieve's wife were left alone in a hut near the Square of Poyntzfield called Christy Ardoch's cottage, when the Captain was meant to be drawing the portrait of the grieve's wife. The evidence from Christy, peeking in through her own window, was not definite but she thought somebody was in the bed. However, the Captain was quoted as saying in defence *"once when we were both there I felt someone coming to the window & I put up the Table to the window to prevent the person Standing there on the outside from looking in upon us but one corner of the window was not covered by the table and I was whilst holding the table up to the window sitting on the Bed."*

The Dancing Master gave evidence to the effect that he had trailed *"Capt Mackinzie going down the Udol avenue on the Mains of Poyntzfield & towards Udol & the grieves Wife following him at a little distance in the same direction, that he followed them on the inside of the hedge beside the avenue, untill they came to a part of the avenue called the* 'cumhagag' *where for a short time he lost sight of them ..."*

The investigation went from bad to worse. A flirting dalliance in the dairy at Poyntzfield could not be confirmed by the dairymaid *"as it was carried on in the English language which she does not well understand."* Evidence was sought from John Urquhart, Footman at Poyntzfield, *"who being interrogated what was his age & did he understand the nature of an oath Replied that he was not quite sure what his age was but thought he might be between eleven & twelve years old & that he did not know what an oath meant."* His evidence was not pursued!

Eventually, the Session found *"that the charge of Adultery alledged against the Female Petitioner is Not proven or brought home to her by the evidence of All or of Any of the aforesaid Witnesses"* but her unguarded behaviour excited suspicion so that they could not grant a certificate clearing her character. Captain Mackenzie escaped reproach.

Donald Sage was later to say that he felt the Session exceeded their powers in becoming involved in this type of case, and clearing defamation became reserved to communicants.

LITERARY RESIDENTS

Although Resolis has produced many distinguished scholars, there are few literary giants associated with the parish.

Sir Thomas Urquhart of Cromarty (*c*1611-1660)

Fortunately Resolis can claim some connection with the great and eccentric Sir Thomas Urquhart of Cromarty, given that Resolis was a significant part of his estates. Urquhart is well served by other works so nothing further need be said here other than to draw attention to one of the finest and most sustained pieces of invective ever committed to print. It was a diatribe in his "*Jewel*" against three ministers of the parishes of which he himself was the patron: Master Gilbert Anderson of Cromarty, Master Robert Williamson of Kirkmichael and Master Charles Pape of Cullicudden!

James Fraser of Brea (1639-1699)

James Fraser wrote some well-received religious books, although it is his "*Memoirs*" that perhaps would intrigue most, giving insight into his ultra-presbyterian views. See Brea in the Gazetteer.

Henry Mackenzie, The Man of Feeling (1745-1831)

William Gordon of Newhall had a great friend in Henry Mackenzie, known as "*The Man of Feeling*" through association with the influential novel of manners of that title written by him.

Mackenzie wrote a marvellous eulogy to William Gordon, who died in 1778 at the young age of 22. The eulogy can be found on a panel within the mausoleum at Kirkmichael and commences:

What science crown'd him, or what genius blest,
No flattering pencil bids this stone attest;
Yet may it witness with a purer pride,
How many virtues sank when Gordon died.

The Reverend Donald Sage (1789-1869)

The "*Memorabilia Domestica*" of The Reverend Donald Sage is famous for its information on Clearances in the far north, but contains much information on his days in Resolis, and is a surprisingly lively read.

Hugh Miller (1802-1856)

Hugh Miller, though not of Resolis, worked within the parish, dallied in the historic site of Castle Craig, and gathered many of his choicest tales from the parish. The reader is directed to his "*Scenes and Legends*" and "*Schools and Schoolmasters*" and to a modern compilation of his newspaper articles "*A Noble Smuggler*," all of which contain Resolis stories.

Angus Munro (*c*1845-1906)

The poetry of Angus Munro of Newhall Bridge gives an unique flavour of parish life at the end of the 19th century, in an era with no television, radio or cinema, but when the village concert reigned supreme. His works would often be sung to a popular tune of the time.

Angus was called upon (one suspects he needed little calling) to provide a poem or a song for just about any event in the area, a wedding – "*On the Occasion of John Walker & Jean Ann Ferguson's Marriage at Ardoch,*" a dance, a funeral, the Laird of Poyntzfield's twenty-first celebration, a departure – "*Lines to Jeannie Munro on leaving home (Poyntzfield) for America.*" Several of his eulogies were printed in the papers of the time – "In *Memory of John Gibb, Free Church Elder, Resolis*" – "*Within Kirkmichael old churchyard, Beside the dust of those he loved, We laid his body down to rest, Until the time his Lord shall come.*"

One of his poems was on the occasion of a concert to raise funds for the Jemimaville water supply in 1887 and looking forward to street lighting:

The folks of Jemima saw their wells getting empty
Put their shoulders together & soon they got plenty
But still they required the expenses to meet
Of digging two wells and pumps to complete
To clear the expense a concert was planned
Which I hope will succeed and meet their demand
The next that is wanted is lamps to give light

To cheer old Jemima on a dark winter night
So I hope you'll succeed with your water & light
Kindly thank all your singers and audience tonight.

David *"Dick"* Cameron (1884-1931)

David Cameron lived at the Resolis crossroads; why he was popularly called *"Dick"* is not known. The house there was occupied by Tom Cameron, who had a shop (*"the Black Shop"*) – a lean-to on the west gable, beside the road. He was gravedigger at Cullicudden. The shop did a good trade in those days before travelling grocery vans, and it sold groceries with sweeties, ham, bread and so on, the business being supplied by wholesalers coming round. My father remembered Mrs Cameron once getting in a good quantity of hard dried fish, and her son Dick being most unpopular when he started calling them *"young sharks."*

Dick built the small extension to the east out of telephone poles from Sheeppark. He drove a post van and repaired bicycles. And he also wrote and published a slim volume of poems sold from the shop and elsewhere. I do not know what sales he achieved, but there are copies of *"Poems by D. Cameron Resolis"* to be found in many of the homes in the parish.

Several of his poems have Resolis locations, such as Castle Craig. Kinbeachie was where he was born and spent his childhood:

The mill now is idle, and gone is the trade,
No water now flows in the tumbledown lade;
The water-rat roams in the broad light of day,
Everywhere ruin and the sign of decay.

The mill and the castle, the burn and the tree,
These are the scenes which in visions I see.
Fain would I rise and return unto thee.
Alas! thou art desolate, fair Kinbeachie.

I understand that local Resolis folk were genuinely touched by the following poem about Cameron's love, from another Cameron family at Badgrinan, *"The Lass o' Badgrinan."*

We met, and a kiss was the seal of our pledge,
And by the clear light of the moon did engage,
To our love to be faithful till Death and aul' age
Pairts me and the lass o' Badgrinan.

Many of Cameron's poems deal with war and national identity, but there are all sorts of oddities – newspapers, the weather and, oddest of them all, influenza:

Address to the 'Flu

O' aches an' pains my banes are fou',
My heid is like tae split in two;
I've got the blastit Spanish 'flu,
    Or spottit fever.
My nose is dreepin' water noo,
    Just like a river.

I sit aboon th' fire an' squirm,
The deil a fit can I get warm;
I spit as thick as ony barm,
    Or drucken slaver.
I canna work, tho' I've a ferm,
    But sit an' haver.

I maune stir oot ower th' door,
Or syne my temp'rature will soar;
I sprauchle in an easy chair,
    My heid fair jumping.
I canna read, I just can sweer,
    Atween my grunting.

David Cameron.

I hae nae will e'en for a draw,
Th' bacca tastes o' rotten straw;
Th' cutty frae my gob'll fa'
    An' lose th' dottle;
Gin I cud mak' th' pub at a',
    I'd swig a bottle.

My wife she says, "There's naething ails ye."
Then what th' deil is this 'at skails me?
An' whiles my very temper fails me
    Tae hear her lauch.
Tho' she may catch it in a whilie,
    Fegs! then she'll cough.

David Cameron died, aged only 46, in Cromarty.

Jane Duncan (Elizabeth Jane Cameron) (1910-1976)

In the central part of the Kirkmichael graveyard stands a small simple stone in memory of Jane Duncan, Author.

In her day, Jane Duncan was a best-selling writer, the most popular of her publications being her "*My Friend*" series of books, although she also wrote complementary books for children. Jane Duncan was born on 10 March 1910, in Renton, Dunbartonshire, and died 20 October 1976, at "*The Old Store,*" Jemimaville.

Her childhood holidays were spent with her grandparents and her much loved Uncle George on the family croft above Jemimaville, looking across Udale Bay to Kirkmichael. The croft, which lies just within the parish of Cromarty, is known as the Colony although in her books she called it "*Reachfar.*"

Having graduated in English from the University of Glasgow, she held secretarial jobs until serving as a Flight Officer (Intelligence) in the WAAF during the Second World War. She lived in Jamaica for 10 years before returning, now a widow, in 1958, to Jemimavillle (the Colony had been sold). Her career as an author was launched in a splash in 1959 with Macmillan announcing it would be publishing seven of her manuscripts with "*My Friends the Miss Boyds*" being the first.

"*Why do you live in a remote place like Jemimaville?* Jemimaville is my place." Jane Duncan used these lines as a chapter heading within her autobiographical "*Letter from Reachfar,*" published in 1975, the year before her death. She regarded the area as her spiritual home, a place from which her creativity sprung.

She drew profoundly upon her own life experiences for her novels. Just from the two pen names she used (Jane Duncan and Janet Sandison) it can be seen

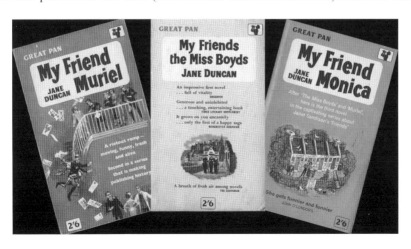

how she weaved reality into her fiction. Her parents were Duncan Cameron (a Police Constable) and Jessie (diminutive of Janet) Cameron ms Sandison.

Elements of her family and friends appear within the characters of her books. Locally there used to be great interest in trying to relate incidents and people in her books to real life. She partly revealed this relationship in *"Letter from Reachfar,"* confirming, for example, that the George of her novels (her last being *"My friends George and Tom"* (1976)) was based on her beloved uncle, George Cameron.

Nowadays her books, once so popular, are hard to find, but it is to be hoped that they will some day come back into fashion. Certainly her children's series, Janet Reachfar, has recently seen a welcome new lease of life in a fresh publication with illustrations by Mairi Hedderwick, herself a passing literary resident of Resolis.

Jane Duncan describes in *"Letter from Reachfar"* an entertaining incident in Jemimaville which captures her style well. She had at this time moved out of a cottage in the village into a converted barn and had lent the cottage for a few days to a Professor of English Literature and his family. Mrs Hart organised a dinner party made up of her family, Jane Duncan, Ian Grimble and the celebrated writer, Neil Gunn. The cottage was surrounded by trimmed privet hedges.

Neil Gunn, when offered a drink, floors the party by asking for some gin, it being expected that whisky would be the great Scot's tipple. Mrs Hart looked embarrassed and Jane Duncan was about to organise bringing some gin in from her house, when the little girls present *"said in unison: 'We'll bring you some gin, Mom,' went out for a second and returned with a bottle three-quarters full of gin. 'Where did you get that?' their father asked, his eyes popping. 'In our garden hedge. There's some more in the back-garden hedge,' they assured Neil Gunn in case three-quarters of a bottle would not be enough."*

Jane Duncan goes on to explain to Neil Gunn that her kind neighbour who trimmed the hedges for her did not *"drink"* while working but always kept an odd bottle of gin or two in the hedges, in the apple trees and in his hen-house in case he became thirsty.

THE ESTATES

Almost all the united parish was, for some of the 16th and 17th centuries, the property of the Urquharts of Cromarty, although estate size varied dramatically with the fortunes of the various branches of the Urquhart family. Other families, such as Rose of Kilravock, Gordon of Invergordon, Mackenzie of Scatwell, Dallas, Duff, Fraser or Lockhart, would pick up estates or portions of estates, intermarry or borrow money on security of land which might then be picked up by the borrower. Further complexity resulted from the tortuous legal arrangements by which land was passed on which led (in the case of several Resolis estates) to many years of legal procedures. Finally, inheritance could be complicated by the surprising number of proprietors who had no legitimate issue (this affecting the inheritance of nearly all the Resolis estates at some time).

The estates in Resolis therefore vary with period, but included Newhall, Braelangwell, Ardoch/Poyntzfield, Kinbeachie, Drumcudden, St Martins and Brea. Each is dealt with separately in the Gazetteer. It should be noted that even Newhall, at its greatest extent, was still a relatively small estate in the context of other estates in the north. Resolis is fortunate in that many of its proprietors took a keen interest in their estate and the welfare of their tenants. Some, however, were not in residence much of the time, or, indeed, ever resident within the parish.

Certain public duties such as new church buildings were charged in proportion to valued rent. Using these valued rent data, I include three snapshots in time, over 300 years, of the relative scale of the different estates.

1718

Sir William Gordon of Invergordon for his Cromartyshire lands within the parish £958-10-0, his lands of St Martin's £93-3-6, his lands of Easter Balblair £100.

Hugh Rose of Kilravock for his lands of Bray and Cullicuddine £467, and for his lands of Craighouse and Toberchurn £106.

Captain Alexander Urquhart of Newhall for his lands within the said united parishes £325.

Charles Urquhart of Brealangwall and Anne McCulloch his Mother for the Lands of Brealangwall £204.

Sir Kenneth McKenzie of Scatwell for his Lands of Wester Culbo £100.

Thomas Urquhart of Kinbeachie £100.

Alexander McKenzie of Belmaduthy for his lands of Easter Culbo £100.

Alexander Duff of Drummuir for his Lands of Drumcuddin £55.3.4.

1801

Charles Lockhart Esqr of Newhall £1,139.15.6½
David Urquhart Esqr of Braelangwell £651.1.8½
George Gun Munro Esqr of Poyntzfield £410.
Sir Roderick Mackenzie of Scatwell Baron for his Lands of Wester-Culbo £100.
John Urquhart Esqr of Kinbeachy £100.0.4
George Mackenzie of Pitlundy Esqr for his Lands of Easter-Culbo £100.
Hugh Robert Duff of Muirtown Esqr. for his Lands of Drumcudden £53.3.0.

1900/1901

Finally, as a more up-to-date snapshot, the figures from the 1900/1901 Valuation Rolls for Resolis are:

Charles F.H. Shaw-Mackenzie of Newhall (Newhall Mansion House and Newhall Mains, Bog of Cullicudden, Muir of Cullicudden, Alness Ferry, Resolis Mains, Springfield, Drumdyre, Ferry, Ferryhouses, East, West and Mid Brae, Kirkton, Woodside, Burnside, Balblair, Agneshill, Fleucherries, Craigton, Toberchurn, Cullicudden Quarry, Sheeppark, Auchmartin, Capernich, part of Chapelton, Henrietta Park, Ferryton, Storehouse) £2,903.1.3
Trustees of Major Colin Lyon-Mackenzie (Braelangwell House and land, St Martins, Mill, Drumcudden Inn) £818.7.6
George Mackenzie Gunn Munro of Poyntzfield (Poyntzfield House, Mains and Mill, Upperwood, Ballicherry, Ardoch, Ballyskilly, Wood of Brae, Tighninnich) £954.7.6
Findon Estate (part of Culbo, Badgrinan, Badgalach) - James Auldjo Jamieson, W.S., and Geo. Dalziel, W.S. £285.10.0
Murdo Macrae and Evan Mackenzie Macrae of Kinbeachie (Kinbeachie Mains Farm, Bruichglass Croft and Inn, Farm of Lower Kinbeachie) £192.0.0
Representatives of the late William Ord Mackenzie of Culbo (part of Culbo) £202.0.0
James Douglas Fletcher of Rosehaugh (Woodhead, Farm of Ardmeanach) £163.13.0
Other Proprietors £438.10.0

The significant proportion of the parish area owned by numerous smaller proprietors in 1900/1901 continued to grow. In 1918, much of Newhall, the largest estate in Resolis, was put up for sale, crofters having the first right to buy; those under simple tenancy arrangements being sold to the highest bidder. A similar process occurred with Findon Estate holdings in Resolis in 1920.

The extant estate houses of Poyntzfield, Braelangwell and Newhall, close together despite the extent of their respective estates, represent some of the best architectural features in the Parish. The other estate houses have vanished.

The three estate houses of Newhall, Braelangwell and Poyntzfield are clustered together within a clearly well-landscaped estate environment. Local roads are not shown; those on the map are the cross-roads with miles from Inverness provided on the road from Kessock Ferry (on the left) and miles from Fort George on the road from Chanonry (on the right). An extract from my personal copy of Plate 61 of Taylor & Skinner's Survey and Map of the Roads of North Britain, surveyed 1775, published 1776.

THE POOR

Those admitted to the Poor's Roll by the Kirk Session were entitled to support, divided into four classes (levels of support) dependent upon their neediness. Thus in 1827 first to fourth classes in Resolis received 10, 7, 5 or 4 shillings respectively.

Funds were raised by weekly church collections and the hiring of either the cheap or the smarter Mort cloth for funerals. The fines of delinquents were also added to the fund. For example, in an 1843 case the fine for fornication is seen to be 15 shillings 6 pence; *"antinuptial fornication"* in many Resolis cases, if accompanied with submission to discipline, resulted in the fine being halved.

There were donations to assist, as in 1827 when Mr Davidson of Tulloch, one of the Heritors, donated £10 – *"The Session considering that meal this year will be very scarce & consequently very dear & that the poor during the summer months will be very destitute resolved that £9 of the above donation should be laid out in purchasing meal for the poor in the month of May."*

Major George G. Munro Esqr of Poyntzfield on 9 December 1833: *"As I am on the eve of leaving the Parish for some time and the appearance of the weather portends a stormy Winter, as you are about distributing the Poors Money, I feel for many excluded from its benefit who are silently suffering & concealing their situation from the world in general; Under this impression I wish to present Ten with a barrel of coals and a Firlot of meal to each which my Grieve will furnish by Monday, in the distribution of which I place implicit confidence in you and Elders discrimination, only I wish so far to confine it to my own Estate, from well knowing the capabilities of the Proprietors of adjacent Estates to support theirs in similar distress:– yet let me not in any singular case cramp your humanity wherever it may be within the Parish:– such case I leave to your discretion, & only regret my limited means compel me to make any such distinctions."*

The Minister thereafter discussed with Colin Mackinzie Esquire of Newhall the principal Proprietor of this Parish respecting the poor on his estate, who *"readily agreed to distribute Meal among them requiring a list of the most needy persons to be sent him as well as the quantity of meal to each that would be thought necessary,"* another 36 indigent parishioners being thereby supplied.

One gift is of particular interest, as in a letter from Thomas Urquhart Esquire of Kinbeachie to the minister: *"London Dec 20th 1832. Dear Sir With this you will receive two pounds for the poor's box which I give on account of the land of the MillBuy apportioned to Kinbeachy and intend to do so annually. When this land was divided to the different Proprietors from which the poor obtained their firing it would only have been justice to them that a certain sum in proportion should have been paid by those who obtained it, annually towards the maintenance of the poor in each parish."*

LISTED BUILDINGS

These buildings were all listed in 1971 or 1981, except for Ferryton Girnal, which was listed in 1989. For Jemimaville Main Street, the following buildings were listed in 1981 as C(S): Bay View, Dale Villa, Drought's Cottage, Friedlander's House, Langlands Cottage, Trenton and Maryville, Laurel Cottage, Rosedene, Woodlands, Firth View, Miss Thomas. Several of these names have changed since listing.

Building Address	Listing Category
Balblair Ferry Inn	C(S)
Braelangwell	B
Castle Craig	A
Ferryton Girnal or Granary	C(S)
Gordon's Mills	C(S)
Jemimaville Main Street, Old Manse (Free Church)	B
Kirkmichael Graveyard Dyke and Gatepiers	C(S)
Remains of Kirkmichael Church and Burial Ground	B
Mains of Newhall	B
Newhall	A
Newhall Gate Piers and Gates	B
Old Cullicudden Burial Ground, Dyke and Gatepiers	B
Poyntzfield Gatepiers, North and South Entrance	C(S)
Poyntzfield House	A
Resolis Manse, Garden Wall and Steading	B
Resolis Free Church	C(S)
Resolis Parish Church	B

It is a pity that none of the distinctive small, stone-built farmsteads of the area has been listed. Very few of these remain in an intact state now, and it would be useful to identify the best preserved of the typical examples that remain.

Note that Category A comprises buildings of national or international importance, either architectural or historic, or fine little-altered examples of some particular period, style or building type, Category B comprises builldings of regional or more than local importance, or major examples of some particular period, style or building type which may have been altered, while Category C(S) comprises buildings of local importance, lesser examples of any period, style or building type, as originally constructed or altered, or simple, traditional buildings which group well with others in categories A and B or are part of a planned group such as an estate or an industrial complex.

GAZETTEER OF RESOLIS

All sites of historical or other significance are provided in this gazetteer. The Gaelic origins of names are given, including different interpretations from alternative sources. The Ordnance Survey grid reference describes the square in which the feature falls and is not rounded.

Achbeag Gaelic: small field.   NH66056475
Named by Annie Fraser about the 1950s; the Reverend Murdo Campbell gave a service on the completion of the new house beside the old crofthouse. One of the skewstones from the old house bears the initials "*WC*" – a family of Camerons lived here.

Achinteppal/Auchinchappel
In Easter Balblair (rentals 1760s-1780s) – presumed to be a field close to the old chapel at Chapelton, given Gaelic *ach* field.

Achmonie   NH65126420
In the late 19th and early 20th centuries, the home of a farming and carpentry family of MacDonalds, "*Billy the Wright*" and son "*Jeemuck the Wright.*" The Post Office moved here from the site now known as Torvaig on the retiral of Mrs Munro in 1947. The first postmistress here was Mrs Christina MacDonald (who had worked in the 1920s for Mrs MacKenzie in the old post office and shop). This was the last Post Office (and shop) in Cullicudden, closing in the late 1960s; the familiar sight of the well-tended red telephone-box disappeared in 2006. Homeguard stores were kept in the shed, a curved building.

Agneshill   NH675627 (general area)
The first reference in Resolis records to Agneshill is surprisingly late, 1811 in the Church Register. The 1812 Braelangwell Estate Plan refers to "*the improvements of Agnes hill,*" although evidence in the Mulbuie Commonty case points to the crofts being established about 1780.

By the 1851 Census, the Agneshill area at 58 people warranted its formation as a separate Enumeration District of the Resolis Census; practically all the heads of families were not born in the parish. Walker states that about nineteen crofts on Agneshill were obliterated by Forestry Commission plantings. The ruins of cottages and farmsteads within the plantations make a poignant sight.

In 1850, three Excisemen raided a bothy containing an illicit whisky still at Agneshill, seizing a copper worm and a barrel of whisky. A band of Agneshill men marched after the Excisemen to battle with them at Auchterflow in a failed attempt to retrieve the whisky. This was a very serious affair. For more than a year afterwards unsuccessful attempts, by day and by night, were made by Dingwall Sheriff Officers to capture the assailants. However, the men slept in different houses in Agneshill each night and would disappear into the woods and moors around Agneshill when notified of the approach of authority.

The Inland Revenue, seeking retribution, grew increasingly impatient with the failures of the Sheriff Officers. Eventually, despairing of them altogether, they sent their own officers out and caught one man later in 1850 and another in 1851, but I have found no record of the others in the case being brought to justice.

Crofting ruins in the forestry at Agneshill.

Allt Dynie *Allt* is burn, but origin of Dynie not known.   NH690635 (one point) A burn (the upper part of which is called Caochan nan Uain (Gaelic: lamb's streamlet) rising in the moor about a mile to the west of Wood of Brae). It runs parallel to, and to the south of, Allt Dubhach, turning into the Ballicherry Burn before joining the Newhall Burn just before Newhall Bridge. There are references to "*Aldiny*" or "*Auldiny*" as a location in 1749 and 1766, and the buildings associated with an area of cultivation are named Auldiny on the 1812 and 1844 Braelangwell Estate Plans just to the south of Braelangwell House. The OSNB records that the burn is known as Allt Dynie "*from the junction of Caochan nan Uain with another small stream, to where it is joined by Allt a Mhadaidh – a distance of about a mile – after which it is known as Ballycherry Burn.*"

Allt Dubhach Gaelic: the blackish burn.   NH672627 (one point)
Rising high in the Millbuie Forest south of Easter Brae, it flows north west,
turning into the Braelangwell Burn before joining the Newhall Burn north of
Braelangwell Mains. Carries the drift geological feature of the Den.

Alness Ferry   NH666658 (general area)
Now distinguished by the unusual sign "*Alness Ferry No Ferry*," this area of
Resolis gained its name from the ferry in relatively recent times. Houses here in
older references fall into the wider definition of Inch, and only gradually did the
term Alness Ferry begin to apply more widely than the ferry itself.

The earliest reference I have found to the ferry is in 1733: "*Catharine
Ferguson Midwife living at the Ferry of Alnes*" in an investigation into the death
of the new-born daughter of Helen Murray in Resolis. Another early reference is
to a marriage on 26 March 1749, linking two ferries, of "*John Holm tenent at ye
ferrie of Alnes & Barbera Gray daughter to Alex^r Gray tenent at ye ferrie of
fowlis*." Subsequent baptism entries show that the groom became the ferrier, *e.g.*
2 July 1755 "*John Holm ferrier Ferry of Alness & Barbara Gray – Alexander.*"

The ferry is shown on maps dated 1794 and 1807, crossing diagonally from
where the remnants of the old pier still exist at Alness Ferry to the seaward point
of the east bank of the Alness River. Donald Sage's son stated: "*Groups of people
also crossed the ferries of Invergordon and Alness from the north on Sabbath
mornings, and took their places in the church of Resolis as regular hearers
during the ministry there of Mr. Sage.*"

The OS (surveying here in 1872) note in the OSNB that at "*the old Alness
Ferry which has been disused for 10 years there is the remains of a Boat Quay
which is not very well defined as some portions of it have been washed away by
the action of the tide.*" This points to closure about 1862.

The only physical evidence remaining of the former ferry now is a raised area
of stones, shingle and seaweed, rich with mussels, projecting into the sea, near
that giant rock and haven of limpets known so prosaically as "*the Big Stone.*" At
the very end of this ancient pier is a large stone with a rusty socket where a ring
to which ropes were once attached used to hang.

Moorground at Alness Ferry was settled in the 1860s/1870s by families from
Wester Ross – McRaes, Mackenzies and Mackays. Resolis Census returns show
many similar resettlements. A note in the family bible by my grandfather Murdo
"*Cute*" reads: "*Duncan McKay my Father came to Alness Ferry in the year May
1864.*" My family arrived from Lochcarron with all their possessions in one cart.

Above Easter Alness Ferry farmhouse, occupied now and for much of the 20th
century by the Holm family, on the tiny burn or ditch that flows eastward
towards Inch, there stood until it was breached in the 1960s a dam which held
back a sizeable volume of water. Willie Stewart, of an old family of Stewart in
Alness Ferry, built the dam, and had a mill with wheels. Amazingly, given the

distance involved, the dam power was brought down to the steading over the intervening ridge by a succession of belts.

A mound at NH670662 in Easter Alness Ferry was investigated as a potential long cairn with inconclusive results.

Alness Ferry/Loch Inch – Four Encampments
NH*c*66656600, NH66776603, NH66656596, and NH66576586.
Nothing now survives of four *"encampments"* noted by the OS in 1875. All four sites were described as being composed of sods and stones about 3 feet high on the outside and 1½ feet on the inside. Reports from visits by archaeologists over the 1950s to 1970s record the loss of these four sites through intensification of cultivation, the fourth site finally being covered by my father's deep litter shed.

Am Bard Loisgte Gaelic: the burnt meadow, near St Martins.
Mentioned by Watson but I have not located any other reference.

An Gnè Gaelic: vein. NH671663 (one point)
A small stream, about 1.5 km long, which rises in Resolis and runs north east until it approaches the farm house of Inch, when it abruptly turns north, and enters the Cromarty Firth, disappearing in some shingle along the high water line.

Arden House NH67946495
The old Schoolhouse at Newmills.

Ardmeanach (see also Mount High). Gaelic: mid-height or the middle ridge.
The old official name of the Black Isle. Ardmeanach was given to Darnley as a wedding present by Mary Queen of Scots. The house in Cullicudden called *"Ardmeanach"* was changed to *"St Teilo*'s" a few years ago. However, the name Ardmeanach lives on as a farmstead at NH701609, also shown on the 1:25,000 1986 Ordnance Survey as Milbuie Crofts, and is given by some nowadays as a name to the forest ridge which runs the length of the Black Isle. The mystery of why Ardmeanach died and the Black Isle thrived awaits solution.

Ardoch Gaelic: *Ard achadh*, high field or high place.
NH710716425 (Poyntzfield, formerly Ardoch) NH71646462 (Ardoch farm)
William Grant of Ardoch built a beautiful burial enclosure in Kirkmichael for his first wife, Florence Dunbar. It is at present in poor condition but its design with stone balusters, carved symbols of mortality and detailed stones is exquisite.

A panel states: *"Grieve not when friends / and kinfolks die / They gain by death eternitie / Heir lyes Agnas Dvnbar / who departit the 18 of Ian 1682."*

Bulloch suggests that the Resolis Ardoch had been owned by a Gordon in the 16th century, for James Gordon of Ardoch and his son George witness, on

7 November 1562, a charter of John Earl of Sutherland, but there are several Ardochs and I suggest confirmatory evidence is required.

The first definite Gordon of Ardoch was Alexander, a younger son of Sir Adam Gordon of Dalpholly. In 1715 he was actively supporting George I, obtaining money and arms for pursuing the Jacobites. In London in the following year, 1716, he killed in a duel the Hon. James Cathcart, son of the 7th Lord Cathcart, for casting aspersions on the courage of his uncle, Sir William Gordon, 1st Baronet of Invergordon. The reports of the duel were biased depending on the side supported, but all indicated the dreadful nature of the combat.

One report stated: *"Mr Gordon receaved five wounds ere the other was touched, and both of them thereafter very eager in their thrusts by a countertang run each other thorow the body. Mr Cathcart's sword entered Mr Gordon's right breast betwixt the niple and the hollow, and went out at his back seven inches, and with the weight of his body in the lounge broke it, leaving 13 inches behind. Mr Gordon entered Mr Cathcart's right breast and went out at his left side, and he endeavouring thereafter to recover his sword, Mr Cathcart, who then threw away what remained of his own, took hold of Mr Gordon's in his both hands, which were cutt when Mr Gordon drew it back."*

Above: Grant of Ardoch Mausoleum in Kirkmichael (photo on right by Andrew Dowsett).
Below: Lady Ardoch's Mausoleum in Kirkmichael (photo by Andrew Dowsett).

Alexander Gordon of Ardoch was one of the parish heritors and frequently appears in the Presbytery records. He married Ann, daughter of Sir Robert Munro, 5th Baronet of Foulis. Sage tells a story about this lady of "*remarkable piety*" known as Lady Ardoch: "*During the greater part of his wife's lifetime, Mr. Gordon was a man of unsettled opinions and of an irreligious life. He was a fond husband, but his affection for the best of wives could not reconcile him to her piety. One evening, on coming home, he found her seated in the parlour with a number of devout persons who were engaging in spiritual exercises. Suddenly he rushed out of the house, and attempted to kill himself. But in an instant the words occurred to him, 'Do thyself no harm,' and from that moment he became a new man. His remaining life was consecrated to the cause of godliness.*"

A most unusual rectangular tomb, of hewn ashlar, was erected above the grave of Lady Ardoch, in Kirkmichael, filled with lime and stone in order to prevent any future interment at the spot. Embedded in the south side of it is a grey freestone tablet (sadly now broken) inscribed: "*Here lies Mrs Gordon, wife of Alexander Gordon of Ardoch, who died in the 75th year of her age. This tombstone is erected to her memory by her nephew Sir Harry Munro of Foulis, Bart., 1768.*"

Alexander and Ann's son, Adam, like his father, took an anti-Jacobite stance. He was captured in 1745 at a skirmish with the Jacobites in Inverurie, reportedly covering the escape of his uncle Captain George Munro of Culcairn. In 1746 he was a lieutenant. Adam, in partnership in the late 1740s with the Cromarty entrepreneur William Forsyth, entered into contracts with the British Linen Company. In 1760 he was a captain in the Earl of Sutherland's Highland Regiment.

Adam had been served heir general to his father in 1753, but did not hold Ardoch long, for "*by minute of sale dated the Twenty ninth day of June one thousand seven hundred and sixty one years Entered into betwixt Captain Gordon of Ardoch on the one part and George Munro Esquire Commissary of Stores for North Britain on the other part*" Ardoch was sold.

George Munro had on 29 May 1760 married the heiress widow Mary Hinde ms Poyntz and became in due course Sir George Gun Munro of Poyntzfield (see Poyntzfield).

The farm of Ardoch, between Poyntzfield and Jemimaville, has been occupied by the same Ferguson family for 150 years.

Auchmartin   NH69776674

Ach is the shortened form of the Gaelic *achadh* for cultivated field, and martin very probably relates to St Martin of Tours, to which Cullicudden church was dedicated.

References to Auchmartin occur in a 1644 Sasine and a 1662 Charter. In a spate of similar erections across Easter Ross and the Black Isle, Auchmartin and

Easter Balblair were erected into part of the burgh of barony of St Martins by Dallas of St Martins (Acts of the Parliament of Scotland, 1 July 1677).

Occupied for many years by the Ferguson family. When farmed by my uncle, James Ferguson, who died in 2000, various remains such as flint tools were found, including a stone axehead found about 1965 at the base of the raised beach.

Auchnintyne and Wester Ballano
Auchnintyne is obsolete, being given in 1580 as a pendicle of "*Ballaiskaillie*" so the location must have been close to modern-day Ballyskelly. Wester Ballano 1580 mentioned in connection with the same but location unknown – it may have been one of the innumerable misspellings in early documents – "*in 1580 King James VI confirmed a charter by Walter Vrquhart sheriff of Crummarty, granting in liferent to Elisabeth Ros (then unmarried), and in heritage to his heirs by her, with remainder to his own heirs otherwise, the towns and lands of Wester Ballano and Ballaiskaillie, with all their pertinents, namely, Auchnintyne and the other pendicles and outsets, in the barony and sheriffdom of Crummarty, in special warrandice of the lands and town of Kinbeachy, with the mill and other pertinents in the same barony and sheriffdom, and to be held of the crown.*"

Badgallach   NH64575987
Gaelic: *am Bard Gobhlach*, the forked meadow.
A farmstead, the first reference to which noted is a 1793 Church Register entry. The farmstead according to the OSNB comprised a cottage of stone and clay-mortar construction, a pen and a corn-drying kiln, although the farmstead is now a ruin. The land was recently sold as an opportunity to re-develop with a crofthouse.

Badgrinnan   NH635601 (general area)
Gaelic: copse of the sunny hillock, or the little wood on the sunny hill.
First reference noted 1702/3. Variant spellings include Badrinan. The **Badgrinnan Burn** immediately to the west forms the parish boundary, flowing north to meet the **Allt Mor**, the boundary following the Allt Mor north east before cutting across to Shoretown.

Badglass and Badlarsin
Badglass is mentioned several times in Rentals and the Church Register, whilst Badlarsin occurs only twice (1769, 1772) in the Church Register; their locations are not known.

Balblair   NH703667 (general area)
Gaelic: *Bail' a bhlair*, farmstead of the plain.
Variants include Belblair 1551, Eistir Belblair 1557. The hamlet increased
dramatically in size with the creation of council housing as Aird Place in the
1960s, named after the local Aird family. Balblair is purely residential; both the
Inn and the Post Office cum shop at its west end are now closed.

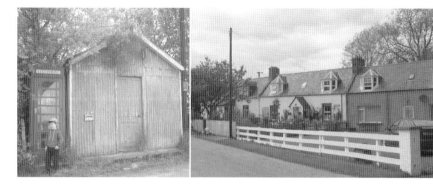

The former Balblair Post Office and the original houses at Balblair.

Balblair-Invergordon Ferry
Balblair Ferry, also called Inverbreckie or Inverbreakie Ferry, was described in
1821 thus: *"Twelve Miles from Dingwall on the North side of the Frith is situate
the populous village of Invergordon, opposite to which is Inverbreckie, and the
Ferry between these places is much frequented by the Inhabitants of the Black-
Isle, and by those who having crossed the entrance of the Beauley Frith at Fort
George, are journeying to Tain, or further Northward. Ferry Piers of the best
kind have lately been completed, that at Invergordon extending one hundred and
thirty-three Yards from High-Water mark; that at Inverbreckie ninety Yards."*

The first reference to its use is in 1664 when Ross of Balnagown went to Rose
of Clava's funeral via *"the ferry of Inverbreakie."*

In 1679, the ferryman, Thomas Urquhart, amusingly refused to get involved
in taking across a group of prisoners to be delivered to the magistrates at
Fortrose, due to fighting amongst factions to force them on or take them off:
*"Upon the morrow .... Urquhart confest. yt. all the boats were secured before ...
McKenzie, prisoners and guard were the lenth of Rosskeen Kirk, and ... being
afloat from the shoar he would let none of ym be brought to it for fear the sd.
John Munro and accomplices and Mackenzie and his companie would kill one
anoyr. the one partie striving to put in ye prisoners, the oyr. to hold ym out."*

In 1780, due to unfavourable winds and tides, Sir John Gordon was unable to
cross from Invergordon to Balblair to go on to Cromarty, and so he hired a boat
from Invergordon to Cromarty.

The piers on both sides were built in 1817 by the engineer Thomas Telford. The Resolis pier is a plain, ramped masonry ferry pier. It is about 100 yards (91 m) long by 7 (6.4 m) or 8 (7.3 m) wide and about 4 feet (1.2 m) high; it does not project to low water mark and is nearly all covered at full tide.

In 1819, the poet Robert Southey visited Invergordon: *"Piers for the use of this ferry, here and on the opposite coast, are nearly finished. Before these were begun passengers were sometimes obliged to mount their horses nearly a quarter of a mile from the shore, and ride mid-leg deep in the water."*

In 1872 it was described as: *"a chartered Ferry between Inverbreakie and Invergordon. It is used for the transit of cattle, vehicles, goods and passengers between Ross-shire and the Black isle. Proprietors Captain McLeod Invergordon Castle and J.S. MacKenzie Newhall House."*

In 1891, there is a report that luggage was left by a traveller on pier at Balblair, to be collected by Inn staff, but half was washed away, presumably not a unique occurrence.

In the early 1940s, the ferry was run by Willie Ross (see picture below), then by Dougal MacIntosh from the mid-1940s to the early 1950s, followed by Ted Abarrow on Dougal's retirement. The final operators (who ran it for many years) were the local family of MacDonald (Sheeppark), but it ceased in the 1990s. The quay is still well used by MacDonald Ferries, which developed significantly to provide services for oil rig and other engineering works around the Firth. Among its boats is the Rosehaugh, one of the two ferryboats that used to serve the Kessock Ferry.

Scott's taxi from Jemimaville on the Balblair ferry; Willie Ross on far left.
Photograph courtesy of Mrs Catriona Gillies.

The influence of the ferry can be seen in the postal addresses given well into the 20th century, as in letters to *"Poyntzfield House, Invergordon."* Saturday was the busiest day for the ferryman, with Resolis folk crossing to the Invergordon shops and returning heavily laden. Resolis ladies would visit the Hairdressing Salon in Invergordon; returning with their hairdo intact via the ferry could be a challenge on a windy, wet crossing. Some pupils from Newhall, including my own mother, went on to Invergordon Academy. My cousin James Holm and I once crossed to give a talk at the Academy one breezy evening, arriving somewhat damp.

Three terraced single-storey cottages behind the pier are incorporated into a shed used by the marine service company now using the pier. They originally were all occupied by ferrymen (1901 Census) but more recently by, east to west, Michael, Summers and Ross families (only Jocky Summers being the ferryman).

The pier in the present-day; the building behind is the converted
ferrymen's cottages; a steep path cuts up the brae to Balblair.

Balblair Ferry Inn   NH70356675

At the top of the brae above the ferry lies the listed Balblair Ferry Inn. In 1999 it closed, the last inn of the parish, ending a tradition of several hundred years.

The three-storey, three bay building was constructed as a roadside hostelry to accommodate travellers with a nearby stable block, a single-storey stone structure with attic space and projecting bays. An advertisement for let in the Inverness Journal, and construction works in the Newhall Estate papers, demonstrate a construction date of 1816 rather than later dates given by other authorities. The building replaced an earlier Inn, but from information from a recent owner, it appears some of the earlier building may have been incorporated within the modern building.

The innkeeper historically was also the ferryman, a convenient combination, in that if a passenger could not cross due to inclement weather, the ferryman benefited as innkeeper. In 1825, a delation for Sabbath profanation was raised by an ancestor of mine, Hugh Ferguson, innkeeper and one of the ferrymen.

While returning from Sabbath evening school, William Thomson and Alexander Fraser had met at Birks two unmarried women, Betty Matheson and Anne Johnson, who were on their way to Sutherlandshire from Inverness, and the party continued to Balblair where Ferguson was asked to send them across the Ferry. "*As the wind was then very high he told them it would be necessary to wait untill the wind fell when he and the rest of the Ferrymen would send them across. That they then came into the house & called for some whisky, after which they ordered supper & some more whisky for Punch ale which they got. That William Thomson called for more whisky which he refused to give them as he considered that they had already as much as was necessary for them & that he*

The former Balblair Ferry Inn in 2006.

did not wish that the evening of the Lords day should be spent in drinking in his house & sent his servant maid Jean Paterson to tell them so. That upon hearing this message William Thomson began to sing & dance upon the floor, upon hearing which he being then in bed resolved to get up & put a stop to such disorderly proceedings by turning them all out but was prevented by his Wife from doing so for fear of a quarrel between them. That the Party being in a room immediately above that in which he was, he called out to them that he would not permit the Lords day to be profaned in his house & that he would make them all answerable for their conduct."

The Session found Thomson guilty of Sabbath Profanation and profane swearing but Thomson would not comply with the punishment to stand before the congregation for public rebuking. It was then determined that Thomson be removed of any church privileges in future (a serious issue when the Poor's Roll administered by the church could be the only protection from starvation in hard times) and be prosecuted for Sabbath profanation before the civil court.

Hugh Ferguson himself was in trouble in 1847. James Grigor, a Cromarty solicitor, sued him successfully for £1.9.6d for expenses caused by his unwise refusal to get out of his bed to carry Grigor across the ferry. His son, "*Hugh Ferguson Junior Ferryman at Balblair,*" in 1850 was accused, but found not guilty, of assaulting David Aird, servant of Poyntzfield, on the brae near the Pier.

There were relatively few cases reported of assault at the Inn itself, compared to other Resolis Inns. In 1853, Mary Munro or Cameron of "*Lanaggan*" Point of Newhall assaulted Margaret Graham, daughter of James Graham, the innkeeper and broke panes of window glass. In 1856, Charles Aird, labourer, Balblair, broke windows at the house of William Graham, Innkeeper at Balblair, and assaulted William Mackenzie, Farmer, Springfield. In 1891, Isaac MacPhee and wife Jane MacPhee, tinkers of No Fixed Abode were drunk and disorderly, the innkeeper being at this time John Campbell. In 1895, the innkeeper, Robert Mackay, was attacked by John Mackay, a crofter in West Ferryton.

Walker gives the following startling tale: "*Another appearance of the devil is said to have taken place at the Balblair Inn, where Donald Sage entertained the Presbytery to dinner after his induction in 1822. Much later in the century, a group of men were drinking and playing cards at the Inn, when a dark stranger appeared and joined them; a card being dropped under the table, they noticed his cloven feet; and on their calling for a Bible, he vanished up the chimney.*"

With the long-term presence of the navy in the Cromarty Firth, and other military operations around the area, there was close examination of activities. A Balblair crofter was fined £2 for failing to observe blackout in January 1915; his wife intervened, and was accused of assault and fined 10/- in turn.

There was pressure on controlling the sale of alcohol around the Firth. In 1918, the Central Control Board (Liquor Traffic) examined the trade of the three remaining Inns in Resolis, and concluded that Balblair was all that was necessary. "*The liquor trade of the Balblair Ferry Inn is carried on in the ground flat of a Farm Dwelling house situated by the roadside. On the upper flat and attics of this building there are a Sitting Room and five Bedrooms. From the letting of part of the house the Licensee has derived an income sometimes as much as £4 per week owing to the great demand for accommodation. There is also a small Grocer's shop situated in a temporary timber-built annexe to the dwelling-house.*" The Board bought out the three licences, retaining (under nationalised control) only Balblair due to its strategic location. Off-sales were "*discontinued except on production of medical certificates, Balblair being only across the ferry from Invergordon.*"

Ballicherry   NH70136455
Gaelic: *Baile a' cheathraimh*, farmstead of the quarter davach.
First reference to the farm noted in the Privy Council Register in 1623.

Balliskelly   NH70436402
Gaelic: *Baile sgeulaidh*, farmstead of the story-teller. Many variant spellings include Bowskaly 1551, Ballaiskaillie 1580 and Balliskilly commonly.

Bardaluich or Burdaluich   NH64056249
Bardaluich is a typical example of an abandoned crofthouse, once home to a family, but now just a ruin with trees growing in amongst the base of its walls and fireplace. To the south west of St Martins Cemetery. The OSNB in 1872 records a Mr R. McFarquhar as the tenant, and states: "*Bardaluich. This name applies to a small farmhouse one storey high, thatched and in middling repair. Captain J. D. McKenzie, Findon, proprietor.*"

Battery   NH650641
On the Ordnance Survey 1905 1:2,500 map, a croft here has the legend "*Battery*" associated with it for an as yet undiscovered reason. On the earlier maps of the 1870s, there is an unnamed building and paddock or kailpatch at this location, with a track leading to its well to the north. A new building was built very close to this site in the late 1980s, called initially "*Fur Elise*" after the Beethoven composition, now "*Firichean House.*"

Birch Cottage / Tigh Beatha   NH66416499
Gaelic: house of life; happily confused with *beith*, Gaelic for birch.
The site of the original Birch Cottage is the first house on the north side of the Cullicudden Straight, at the east end. The first reference I have found to the house as named Birch Cottage is in 1924; it was occupied by a Fowler family in the 19th century. Now named Tigh Beatha, with the name Birch Cottage applied to another cottage close by to the west.

Birks or Birkis

Gaelic: *a Bheithearnaich*. "*Birk*" is an old northern name for birch.
Part of the Poyntzfield Estate. Strangely, though the name Birks frequently occurs in the records (starting with a reference in a 1551 Charter and included within early Census returns), it is seen in a modern context only in the "*Burn of Birks.*" This flows down from Mount High to its confluence with Ballicherry Burn close to Ballicherry itself. As there are many records of tenants, smiths, weavers and so on at the Birks (*e.g.* 1786 "*Hugh Barnet wright in the Birks of Poyntzfield*") it is surprising that the name now is not in use.

There are historical reports of an Inn associated with the Birks, and indeed a newspaper advertisement of 1826 for Poyntzfield Estate includes "*Birks with Inn attached to it.*" However, little is known about this Inn. The tenant farmer at Birks in the early 19th century was Hugh Cameron, and there is an 1833 court reference to his non-payment of debt for beer having been delivered and sold, so it is likely that the Inn was operated by the farmer at the Birks himself.

Black Ditch (Henrietta Park)   NH68596566

The derelict crofthouse (whimsically juxtaposed with Castle Craig on the cover) at Black Ditch was last lived in by Andrew Whyte, who left in 1957. The land and steading has been in the ownership of the Holm family of Easter Ferryton. It is not known which watercourse is referred to by Black Ditch, possibly the Camilty Burn at the bottom of the brae.

Blarakey

Located in the Newmills area, and referred to in documents dated 1741, 1755 and 1776 but not now known.

Blernaclach (and variants such as Blairnaclach)

Although mentioned in the Church Register in 1749 and a Charter in 1766, Blernaclach has vanished.

Brae   NH662628 (general area)

Gaelic: *braigh*, upland. Variants: Brey, Brea.
A long established estate in Resolis, the "*Lands of Brey*" mentioned in a 1506 Sasine is certainly the Resolis Brae, although it has been argued that the commonly referred to "*Lands of Brehe*" in a 1349 document may not be the Resolis Brae. Regardless, this was part of the early Urquhart holdings in Resolis. In 1599 Thomas Urquhart was served heir to his grandfather Walter Urquhart sheriff of Cromerthie in the 5 oxgangs of the lands of Brey in the lordship of Ardmanach, of the old extent of £4.40. In 1617 the same lands were resigned by John Urquhart in favour of James Fraser (son of Lord Lovat), who became Sir James Fraser of Brey, dying in 1649. His son James (1639-1699) became the

famous covenanting divine, James Fraser of Brea. Nowadays, there are houses, west to east, at Wester Brae, West Brae, Brae Farm and Easter Brae, but it is the farmhouse at West Brae that is the site of the *"Old House of Brae."*

Sage, writing in 1836, states: *"The house in which he was born in 1639 is still standing, and is occupied at present by a tenant on the estate of Newhall. Several passages of Scripture are carved, in capital letters, on the west gable."* In contrast, the OS in the 1870s recorded that the materials of the old house of Brae had been re-used in erecting other buildings in the vicinity, and the farmhouse on the site itself had, above the door, a stone built in with *"16 D.F. I.F. 82"* cut on it, and, on the west gable, a triangular stone, surmounted with a fleur-de-lis, with inscription *"Fear God."* The RCAHMS states: *"At NH656621 lies the site of the* 'Old House of Brae' *destroyed in 1682. A carved stone reading* 'Fear God' *is let into the SW gable of the present building, a single-storey cottage, built in 1894."* The RCAHMS presumably based their record on other details on the stone, which is still the original, being triangular and surmounted by a fleur-de-lis, and reads, in full, *"1682 / REBUILT / 1894 / FEAR GOD."* See page i for photograph.

James Fraser at an early age became very religious, and obtained licence as a preacher of the gospel from a presbyterian minister in 1670. He was ordered to be apprehended as a preacher at conventicles (unauthorised meetings of Covenanters) in 1674. He was imprisoned on the Bass Rock for two and a half years, being released on security for good behaviour in 1679. While in prison he studied Hebrew and Greek, and gained knowledge of oriental languages.

In 1681 he was again arrested and committed to Blackness Castle as a prisoner until he paid a fine of five thousand marks and gave security either to give up preaching or quit the kingdom. A brother-in-law caused the fine to be remitted, and Fraser was sent out of Scotland. In 1683 he was ordered to be imprisoned for six months in Newgate, London, for refusing the Oxford oath.

Despite these tribulations for his strongly Calvinistic views, Fraser eventually returned to Scotland and practised as a minister and was even a member of the assemblies of 1690 and 1692.

In addition to all this, Fraser had time to marry twice and write several religious books and his memoirs. He had two daughters, and in the absence of a son, the son of his elder daughter (she married Hugh Rose, fifteenth Baron of Kilravock), James Rose, succeeded to the lands of Brea.

Fraser's posthumously published *"Memoirs"* gives a blow-by-blow and fascinating account of his conversion and the pains he suffered for his beliefs. From the very start of his Memoirs, his character is revealed:

"1. I was born in the North of Scotland, in 1639, July 29th, and was not like to live, but the Lord healed me: for the evil humours broke out in boils great and numerous, so that I was very wholesome thereafter; my disposition was sullen, and I loved not to be dawted, nor to wear gaudy clothes; nor had I any wise tales like other children, so that I gave no occasion to my parents to repeat them, as parents usually do with fondness: for though my parents were fond enough of their children, yet my temper was so peevish, that I was no dawtie; only at school I learned well, though now and then I stayed away.

2.   Even at this time I showed plainly that I had a will to do evil; for the seeds of wickedness did spring up, and appeared in many vicious, childish tricks ..."

The Brae area is particularly rich in prehistoric remains. A scheduled long cairn lies at NH661628, immediately west of Easter Brae farmsteading. This long cairn, composed of large stones, has been robbed of stones and mutilated by the foundations of old crofts. It appears to have been about 70 m long and 12.5-15 m wide. It has a chamber at the west south west end and may have had a second chamber at the east north east end. A second scheduled cairn lies 10 m south of the long cairn at NH661627, measuring 6.5 m in diameter over a kerb of boulders, and has been robbed at the centre. It is an unchambered round cairn. Other potential cairns have been identified at NH660627.

Another scheduled, wedge-shaped long cairn lies at Wester Brae, at NH656613, disturbed by a forestry track but now accessible following forestry felling. Again, it is oriented east north east – west south west and is 25.9 m long and 11.6-14.6 m wide. It lies in an area of a field of small cairns. Hut circles and a field system are found at NH653617 within the remains of an extensive cairnfield, damaged by agriculture and afforestation. A further cairnfield at NH685619 was lost within a fir plantation.

Braelangwell Listed   NH69496425

A hybrid– Gaelic: *braigh*, an up-land, and Norse: *langvollr*, long-field, giving *"the upland long-field."*

The first written reference I have found to the Resolis Braelangwell is in a 1576 Charter. In 1577 King James VI confirmed a grant of the liferent of Bralangall in the sheriffdom of Cromartie by Walter Vrquhart sheriff of Cromartie to his wife Elisabeth Makkanze. Thomas Urquhart obtained Braelangwell 1670-72, and died in 1685. He was the brother of the first Alexander Urquhart of Newhall, and had been the Minister of Dipple and then of Essil before being deposed in 1663 for not submitting to the church government. The son of Thomas, Colonel William Urquhart of Braelangwell, is buried in Kirkmichael.

His memorial has a startlingly three-dimensional skeleton and other symbols of mortality. *"Here lyes the dust of William Urquhart / of Brealanguell / son to Mr Tho. / Urquhart & Henreta Duglas of / worthie memorie who was born at / Esle in Morray the* [space] *day of March / 1660 & died at Brea. 16 Decr 1708 / Generally beloved in his life for his / uprightness & greatlie regreated his / death -Phi- To me to live is Christ & to / die is gain -Rev-Blessed are the dead who / die in the Lord - Thy dead men shall live / together with my dead bodie shall they arise / awake and sing ye that dwell in dust -Psa- /*

Surely he shall live for ever the / righteous shall be in everlasting remembrance."

His son Charles Urquhart of Braelangwell (1699-1776) is also buried at Kirkmichael. David Urquhart of Braelangwell (1748-1811), the son of Charles, built the current Braelangwell House and made many improvements to the estate. He married twice, in 1786 Henrietta Gordon of Newhall (died 1799, buried Kirkmichael), widow of Thomas Lockhart, and in 1804 Margaret Hunter (died 1839), joint heritor of her brother, a wealthy Edinburgh merchant.

Colonel Charles Gordon Urquhart of Braelangwell (1788-1828), the only son from that first marriage, was unmarried when he died when a shed collapsed on him in Greece, on the island of Karabusa where he was Governor. Formerly an officer in the Scots Greys, he had sold the estate with the exception of a small portion including the ancient burying ground of Kirkmichael, which, having descended in strict tail, became the property of his half-brother David. David Urquhart was born at Braelangwell, the second son of David Urquhart of Braelangwell, by his second wife, Miss Hunter. His father died while David was still a child, and he was brought up by his mother. He had a military career in the Greek service and thereafter was given important diplomatic positions, including several in Constantinople, and wrote much on politics and travel. He was responsible for the naturalisation of the Turkish bath in Britain through his enthusiastic report in his *"Pillars of Hercules"* in 1850 and subsequent lectures. He died in 1877.

Above, Braelangwell House.
Left, memorial in Kirkmichael to Colonel William
Urquhart of Braelangwell (1660-1708).

In reality, however, Charles and David, despite their title, had little to do with Braelangwell, as their father had died in 1811 and most of Braelangwell was rouped in 1812, coming into the possession of the family of Fraser. In 1836 Sage describes Braelangwell as belonging to Duncan Davidson, Esq. of Tulloch, being a small property once highly improved, but of late much neglected.

Braelangwell House has two storeys and five bays. It was built in the late 18th century by David Urquhart of Braelangwell, but was later enlarged and given a new ashlar seven-bay front to the south, with Ionic-columned porch, in 1839-1844 or 1845, its 18th century front still visible to the east. A large courtyard steading, c1800, and dovecot, lie to the rear at NH693644.

General Sir Hugh Fraser was in the thick of the action during the 1843 Resolis religious disturbances. Despite the fact that Shaw-Mackenzie of Newhall was the patron of the Church of Resolis, and was present, it was from Braelangwell House that the Presbytery, accompanied by a party of gentlemen and ladies, set out to induct the new minister against fierce local opposition. The previous minister, Donald Sage, had left the Established Church for the Free Church. Sir Hugh Fraser had a pistol which he received from one of the Coastguard; although he later claimed he did not fire it, certainly shots were fired. He was closely involved with the arrangements for the considerable numbers of special constables deployed during the disturbances.

His carriage was subsequently stoned near Invergordon. His massive granite memorial in Kirkmichael collapsed face-down in the turf. It reads: "*Sacred to the memory of Lieutenant General Sir Hugh Fraser, K.C.B. of Braelangwell and of the Madras Army, who died at Braelangwell, on the 6[th.] day of October 1851, aged 79 years. And also to the memory of Dame Isabella Fraser, his wife, who died at Braelangwell, on the 12[th.] day of August 1852, aged 55 years. Those who knew them best, were those who regretted them most deeply. May they rest in peace.*"

In 1836 Sage states: "*There is a distillery in the parish, at the place of Braelangwell, famed for excellent whisky.*" The distiller (and farmer at the Mills and Mains of Braelangwell) was George Andrews, from Banff; it appears from various civil proceedings that the enterprise was fraught with financial problems. There were workmen's barracks to serve the distillery, and it is reported in 1832 there was even an Officer of Excise in residence.

It is recorded in 1813, that David Urquhart "*some years ago, established a mill for carding wool, and jennies for spinning it, also a wauk-mill, two flax-mills, and a flour-mill. After encountering all the difficulties by which new plans are always attended, he has now the satisfaction of seeing them answer the purposes for which he intended them. Mr Urquhart has planted an orchard of thirteen acres, which is the only one of consequence in the north.*"

An advertisement from 1821: "*TO FLOUR MILLERS. An uncommonly favourable opportunity now offers for a respectable Person of the above description, to join in a flourishing Concern, where there are Flour, Meal, and Barley Mills in full employ, and possessing every advantage as to Machinery and Land. This Notice is only addressed to Millers possessing a thorough knowledge of their business, and of some capital. Particulars will be communicated, on personal application alone, to Mr. James French, Flour Mills of Braelangwell, near Cromarty."*

The mills at Braelangwell had at least two separate locations. The 1812 Estate Plan shows a mill dam close to Braelangwell House, with a flour mill on the west side of the Ballycherry Burn close to Ballycherry itself. However, the 1844 Estate Plan shows a new mill dam much closer to the Newhall Burn, with a lade passing what must be a relocated mill right beside the Newhall Burn.

Walker states that the Lady's Bridge and Road were constructed to enable Florence (actually Flora) Mackenzie in Braelangwell (a niece of Colin Mackenzie Dhu, married James Lyon Merchant of Inverness in 1797), to visit her brother at Newhall. Her son, Colin Lyon Mackenzie of St Martin's and Braelangwell, became Provost of Inverness.

In a wood at Braelangwell (see page vii for photograph) there is a surreal sight: a substantial *"Bridge to Nowhere"* – the bridge over the Braelangwell Burn, built for the abandoned railway line. A length of the light, steel track protrudes from the burn.

Braeview   NH653637

A 20 acre croft occupied in the late 19th – early 20th century by Camerons and then, from about 1920, by Mackenzies, moving from the crofthouse now known as Cullicudden Croft. Andrew Mackenzie was the mailman; he went to Conon every day in a gig to collect the mail; for no reason now known, his son Alexander was known as *"The Weasel"* and his grandson Alistair as *"The Monkey."* The land was taken over by Nicol of Culbo and the crofthouse is now just a ruin.

Bruichglass   NH62196211

Gaelic: green brae or slope.

Immediately to the east of the Shoretown road, where two trees grow, to the west of the modern house signed *"No. 1 Kinbeachie,"* there once stood a public house and shop (the buildings can be seen on early OS maps). It is likely that this location would have served passengers of the Foulis Ferry, the landing point of which was not far away, as well as local residents.

From Valuation Rolls, James Macdonald was the last Innkeeper, for in 1915/16 he is listed as the Innkeeper at Bruichglass whilst in 1916/17 the building is described as *"Old Inn"* and condition *"Ruinous."* James Macdonald, who ran the pub and shop, was known as *"Exactly"* from his habit of invariably adding, when telling a customer the cost of an order, *"Exactly."*

There are few records of the Inn, except, almost inevitably, in criminal cases. In 1859, when Hector Ross was the innkeeper, Hugh McLachlan, Shepherd, Kinbeachie, was prosecuted for assault on Alexander Jack, Farmer at Woodhead, in the inn. The following year, William McLennan was fined 10s for malicious mischief, and again in the same year, John McMillan, shepherd, assaulted Alexander Stewart, farmer, Brae.

In 1864, a case of slander involved the two inns of Bruichglass and Drumcudden. Catherine Gordon and husband Donald Fraser, innkeeper and farmer, Drumcudden, claimed Janet Ross (wife of Hector Ross, innkeeper and farmer, Bruichglass) had given whisky to Donald Fraser with wicked intent, and that the said Donald Fraser had carnal connections with Janet Ross. The slanderous statements were made before Ann MacDonald, servant, Drumcudden, Donald Forbes, Cullicudden, and other witnesses.

In 1880, when Alexander MacDonald was the innkeeper, John MacKay, salmon fisher or labourer, Toberchurn was fined £1 for malicious mischief, he having broken eight windows and damaged a sewing machine, by throwing stones and other vessels at the windows. In 1905, Alexander Jack, farmer, Easter Shoreton was fined £1 for being drunk and disorderly in the inn, at that time still occupied by Alexander Macdonald.

Burnside (at Newhall; not the house in Jemimaville)   NH695652
Gaelic (Watson): *Tigh an daimh*, ox-house.
The first reference found is in 1741 (Church Register). The OS in 1872 recorded: *"Burnside. This name is applied to a Croft house, two storeys high, having outbuildings attached all being thatched and in very good condition."*

Camilty Burn   NH685655 (one point)
Gaelic: *Camalltaidh*, crooked little burn.
The burn flowing east from Fanny's Brae, taking a clearly man-made 90 degree turn north east of Newhall House to reach the Newhall Burn near Shawfield. The original course of the Camilty can only be conjectured. Could it have once flowed down near the current Newhall House to feed the original Mill of Newhall (shown on a 1788 estate plan as close to the current entrance way)?

Capernach or Capernich Gaelic: *Ceaparnaich* or *a' Cheaparnaich*, an extension of *ceap*, a block, whence *ceapach*, tillage plot.
The name of Capernach is no longer in use, but the lands of Capernach have been referred to in Resolis documents (*e.g. "boig of Capparach"*) since 1658, are shown on Estate Plans and even feature on the Valuation Roll up to 1930. In the Sale Particulars of the Estate of Newhall of 1918 excluded from sale were *"The lands of Gordons-mill, including Capernach and Whisky Park."* The lands of Capernach were to the immediate north east of the current Newhall Smiddy.

Castlecraig or Craighouse – Tower-House   NH63196381
Listed Scheduled. Gaelic: *Tigh na creige*. For photograph, see front cover.
Easily the most striking building within Resolis, Castle Craig, set against the
backdrop of the Cromarty Firth, catches the imagination of all who view it. Hugh
Miller loved the ruin and, despite its severely eroded and damaged condition,
there is hope yet that it may be rescued before final collapse.

Technically, it is a 15 m high rectangular towerhouse, the west wall ruinous,
the east gable with corbelled parapet walk linking the corner turrets, all within a
ruined courtyard. There is a door in the gable on to the parapet walk.

The loss of the west wall shows the interior in cross-section, the stone
vaulting on each floor still in place, although the stairs up which Hugh Miller
once climbed have long gone.

The site, approached from Craigton down a slope from the south, is a roughly
rectangular promontory with steep drops to the north, east and west. The
perimeter has been enclosed by a wall, the house itself forming part of the
enclosure on the south. The wall, now very fragmentary except for a north
stretch pierced with gunloops, has had a battlement and projecting round towers.

It was built before 1561, when the lands of Craig *"cum fortalico"* were
granted by the Bishop of Ross to Thomas Urquhart of Culbo, and an early 16th
century date seems likely.

Walker states that it is believed that Craighouse was confiscated by the
Church prior to the Reformation due to Urquhart misdemeanours, and to have
become the principal seat of the Bishops of Ross. It was occupied in 1563 by
Donald Munro, formerly High Dean of the Isles, and in the Reformed Church,
Commissioner for planting Kirks in Ross-shire. Sage, in 1836, wrote that: *"An
ancient document is now in the Museum of the Antiquarian Society at Inverness,
presented by Colin Mackenzie, Esq. of Newhall. It is a warrant signed by the
Bishop of Ross, and dated at Craighouse, his residence; in virtue of which
certain persons were to be pursued and incarcerated for violently resisting the
possession of the place of Tolly, near Dingwall, to whom the bishop granted a
lease of it."* I have been unable to locate where this document is currently stored.

The property passed through several Urquhart hands. Alexander Urquhart of
Craighouse married twice; his second wife, Lilias Dallas, subsequently married
Alexander Urquhart of Newhall. Her son by her first husband was John of
Craighouse, M.P. for Cromartyshire in 1693. He seems to have left what he
could to his half-brother George, son of Lilias Dallas by Alexander Urquhart of
Newhall. This George was of Greenhill, Cromarty, but in one charter is also
designated as of Craighouse. He made a fortune during the prosperous period of
the herring fishery, but his sons did not survive him, and the male line of this
branch died out.

A letter exists, to Sir John Urquhart of Cromarty, dated 6 March 1664: *"To the
Sheriff of Cromarty, from his mason. The House of Craighouse was parged*

within on Tuesday last, and I intend, in the strength of the Lord, to be there, laying the hall floor, on Sat. John Urquhart, Your honour's servant, to his most loving master."

For many years it was part of the Newhall estate, before being gifted to the Chief of Urquhart, an American. At time of writing, the current Chief of Urquhart had initiated the formation of a trust to facilitate conservation of the building.

Hugh Miller states (in My Schools and Schoolmasters) that he "*passed whole hours among the ruins of Craighouse, – a grey fantastic rag of a castle, consisting of four heavily-arched storeys of time-eaten stone, piled over each other, and still bearing a-top its stone roof and its ornate turrets and bartizans,*

– A ghastly prison, that eternally

Hangs its blind visage out to the lonely sea.

It was said in these days to be haunted by its goblin, – a miserable-looking, gray-headed, gray-bearded, little old man, that might be occasionally seen late in the evening, or early in the morning, peering out through some arrow-slit or shot-hole at the chance passenger. I remember getting the whole history of the goblin this day from a sun-burnt herd-boy, whom I found tending his cattle under the shadow of the old castle-wall. I began by asking him whose apparition he thought it was that could continue to haunt a building, the very name of whose last inhabitant had been long since forgotten. 'Oh, they're saying,' was the reply, 'it's the spirit of the man that was killed on the foundation-stone, just after it was laid, and then built into the wa' by the masons, that he might *keep* the castle by coming back again; and *they're saying* that a' the verra auld houses in the kintra had murderit men builded intil them in that way, and that they have a' o' them their bogle.'"

On a much later visit, Miller found that "*the huge kitchen chimney of the building – a deep hollow recess, which stretches across the entire gable, and in which, it is said, two thrashers once plied the flail for a whole winter, – bore less of the stain of recent smoke than it used to exhibit twenty years before; and inferred that there would be fewer wraith-lights seen from the castle at nights than in those days of evil spirits and illicit stills, when the cottars in the neighbourhood sent more smuggled whisky to market than any equal number of the inhabitants of almost any other district in the north. It has long been alleged that there existed a close connection between the more ghostly spirits of the country and its distilled ones.*"

Cavin, the pecks of Meikle and Little Caleshie, the peck of Crostenhallach

Cavin (Gaelic: smooth pass) is mentioned by Watson and Walker and occurs in the 1889 Valuation Roll. A 1694 document refers to the Oxgate of Lorgan, the peck of Crostenhallach and the pecks of Meikle and Little Caleshie. All these names are defunct.

Chapelton and Chapelton Point (and Newhall Point)   NH709671

Gaelic: *Bail' an t-seipeil.*

The name of Chapelton or Chapeltown surprisingly does not appear until fairly late in the records, the first occurrence thus far found being within the 1798 Militia List. Whilst the hamlet along the shorefront, and the land behind it, is Chapelton, there is Chapelton Farm, there is Chapelton Cottage, and the Point here is given as either Newhall Point or Chapelton Point depending upon source.

There was a wooden pier at Chapelton, near the Craggan, in the early decades of the 20th century, utilised amongst other things for shipping timber. One contract involved shipping the timber from Culbo Wood. This pier was utilised as a cheaper alternative for collection of coals by local families than the ferry pier, but was reputedly very dangerous to operate a horse and cart from.

In 1985, the local planning authority, somewhat surprisingly, granted planning permission for a new house at Chapelton Point on an ancient graveyard.

There was excellent evidence for the remains of a chapel and burial ground at Chapelton. Firstly, a chapel is shown on the early Ordnance Survey maps and their surveyors reported in the 1870s: *"This is said to be the site of a Roman Catholic, therefore presumably Pre-Reformation, chapel, about which nothing further is known. When the area around the chapel was trenched* 'large unchiseled stones' *were uncovered. These were assumed to be grave-stones."* Secondly, a rectangular chapel and a surrounding circular area of associated land are shown on the earlier 1852 map of the Balblair area produced for the Graham *v* Disher case. And thirdly, Walker's booklet on Resolis states: *"At Newhall-point human bones were once discovered when digging behind the Craggan House."*

Despite this, permission was granted and inevitably archaeological investigations in the form of rescue excavations initiated. These revealed a Christian Cemetery in use during the 11th and 12th centuries (Reed, 1995).

Curiously, two of the better-preserved skeletons disappeared from the site late in 1985, never to re-appear. There are several theories still current in the parish as to the culprits. The remaining skeletons were reburied within the original

Chapelton from the Point, looking up the Firth to Ben Wyvis.

burial site by the local minister in 1986, and the site was scheduled as a monument of national importance in 1989.

The findings from the excavated areas (representing only part of the site) showed that the cemetery was probably originally circular. No artefacts were found in the graves, as expected with Christian burials. Thirty eight graves were positively identified, and it was suggested that more than 200 may lie within the cemetery as a whole; skeleton survival had been very variable, from fair condition to mere stains in the sand. The heads of many bodies were flanked by crudely-worked, sandstone block head-sets. The graves were packed densely together, and the graveyard may have been abandoned following perhaps two or three centuries of use when all the space within the enclosure was used up.

Only part of the site was investigated, and the investigator thought it likely that a small stone or wooden chapel is located elsewhere within the enclosure.

In 1986 a stone support for what possibly was a free standing cross was found whilst digging a garden adjacent to the excavated area. A geophysical survey of the field to the south of the medieval cemetery site in the 1990s showed likely graves and possible structural features.

Newhall Point – Icehouse (Chapelton Point)   NH70866705

A large vaulted single-chamber icehouse built into the slope at Newhall Point in 1837 survives as a relic of the once prosperous local salmon-fishing industry. Walker states that the Newhall Point salmon stake nets yielded an annual rental of £600 and produced about 3,000 fish annually.

The fish were shipped to London, using ice from the ice-house to keep them fresh. Ditches were blocked during frosty weather so that ponds would form and freeze, and farm servants would break and gather the ice, and feed it in through the 1.2 m square opening on the brae-face side of the roof. It has been suggested that, 60 cm thick though the walls are, insulation between the ice and the wall was also used. The ice could be preserved in this way until August or September.

The size of the ice-house, which is of red sandstone, impresses you once you are inside: internally it is about 9.1 m long by 4.6 m wide, with the arched roof rising to 5.5 m at its highest point. For photographs, see page 6.

Chetwood   NH658642

Once occupied by the Matheson family, this crofthouse is now demolished.

Cnoc nan Taibhsean – see under Inch.

Cnoc Topach   NH662639 (general area)

Gaelic: hillock of the top or tuft (OSNB).

Close to, and sometimes included within, the area of Springfield, Cnoc Topach on modern maps lies to the north west of Springfield. There were many variants of the name, the most extreme being Knocktobark (in the Church Register in 1744, its earliest mention).

Corry or Corrie

The settlement of Corry was known under many variants including Corrie (1644 and 1662), Cory (*c*1637 and 1654), Correy (1677), Quarry (1750), ye Quarie (1756), Quorrie (1757) and Quorie (1760), but the name has now disappeared. It is shown near Ardoch in the 1654 Blaeu map of the area, and indeed is described in 1767 in the Church Register as "*Quarie of Ardoch.*" A 1730 document refers to: "*All and haill the Crofts and particats of Land called Corry And All and haill the Town and Lands of Birkis and East Audynie.*" The name lives on in Resolis as "*the Corrie,*" the house on the bend at the east end of the Cullicudden Straight, or, as originally named around 1948, "*the Corry.*"

Craggan   NH709671

Craggan appears as a place name on the Kirk Session Records in 1822. Several houses at Chapelton are described as Craggan in the 1918 Sale Particulars of the Estate of Newhall, but "*Craggan House*" lies at NH709671.

Masons called Mackenzie were long associated with the land and buildings now known as Craggan. There was a 1799 feu contract between the landowner Charles Lockhart and Thomas McKenzie Mason, who built two houses, one byre and one barn, with a feu rent of 10 shillings yearly. In 1839 Thomas McKenzie Mason Chapleton sold the property for £49 to his son Thomas McKenzie Mason Inverness. In 1852 there was a General Service Specification in favour of William McKenzie Mason son of Donald McKenzie Mason brother german of late Thomas McKenzie who died in 1844 and in 1853 there was an Instrument of Sasine in favour of William McKenzie Mason. The McKenzie family continued to own the property well into the 20th century.

Craggan House was the home for many years of the local haulage contractor Hugh Fraser and his family ("*H. D. Fraser & Sons.*") The motto of the firm emblazoned on all their lorries was "*Any ware Anywhere,*" raising a smile from expatriate Resolis folk across Britain whenever one of the distinctive green and cream lorries was spotted.

Craigton   NH635637

The cluster of houses and farm above Castle Craig. A new footpath now leads down from Craigton to the shore and the castle. Craigton's farmer in the 1930s, Alexander McLennan, had a nickname strange even for Resolis – "*Hellmajaw*" McLennan received his unusual alias due to his complaints of a sore tooth.

Crossroads, Resolis and War Memorial   NH66716517

In the 1914-18 war, the only newspaper in the parish came to the shop at the

Crossroads, and people would gather for the news. The newspaper was often read out to the company.

About 1930, a local haulier named Bowie built a garage at the Crossroads at the top of the Church Road, a new venture. A petrol pump was installed, with great difficulty as the pressure kept pushing the tank out of the ground. The local bus service started with the garage here; the earliest bus still had metal stanchions for cow tie-chains on it, demonstrating its origins. Apparently, the bus was run on such a shoestring budget that it could not depart until the fares were collected to buy petrol for the journey. A bicycle shop was opened by Andrew Whyte (of Blackditch), and this proved to be a focal point for young people on Saturday nights.

The distinctive grey granite War Memorial at the north east corner of the Crossroads was unveiled in 1921 in front of more than 300 people. It is a poignant reminder of how many lives were prematurely taken in the two World Wars – 20 in the First, and 13 in the Second – out of the small rural population of the parish. Early on 14 November 2008, a car smashed through the fence to the west of the site, ran 70 m through a field, burst through a gate and demolished the memorial, the young male driver surviving relatively unscathed. At time of writing, funding for repair and re-erection was being sought.

Culballachie
There are many references to Culballachie in the Church Register in the 1750s. Located on Braelangwell Estate, beside the Newhall Burn. Spelled Culballachie on a Sasine in 1762, Kilnwallachie on 1812 estate plan, and Coul Ballachie on 1844 Estate Plan. Not in current common usage.

Culbo   NH640610 (general area)
Variants: Eistir Culbo 1557, Eistir and Wastir Culboll 1560; from Norse: *kula*, a ball or knob, and *bol*, a farm-stead, hence farmstead on the rounded hill.
The ownerships of Easter and Wester Culbo followed different routes. The land belonged to the bishop of Ross as part of the patrimony of the bishopric, and, in the 1550s-1570s, parcels of land, separately containing Easter and Wester Culbo, were passed around the family (at that time the Leslies).

Families thereafter associated with Easter Culbo included those of "*Thomas Vrquhart the son of the deceased Alexander Vrquhart sheriff of Crombathy*" and his relations, the Dallas family (who included the Dean of Ross and the Commissary Clerk of Ross), and the Mackenzies of Pitlundie and Culbo.

Families thereafter associated with Wester Culbo included those of Colin Mackenzie of Kintail, Sir Robert Farquhar of Moyness, Sir John Urquhart, Ross of Pitkerrie and the Mackenzies of Scatwell.

Interestingly, within all this, there is a 1667 Disposition which states that certain lands belonging to Sir James Fraser of Brey in 1649 were appraised by

James Lauder of Edinburgh and disponed to Major George Bateman of Dalcross in 1666. These lands included many in Resolis including *"Culboes – of auld called Cubusches"* which raises a question as to the Norse origins of the name.

Sage in 1836 reports on the two: *"East Culbo, the property of Dr M'Kenzie, occupied until very lately by small tenants, but all of whom are now removed, and the whole property thrown into a large farm, which Dr M'Kenzie has highly and judiciously improved by trenching and planting"* and *"West Culbo, a part of the estate of Sir James W. M'Kenzie of Scatwell, Bart. on which no improvements have been made."*

George Mackenzie, of the Mackenzies of Belmaduthy, obtained Easter Culbo in 1721 (sasine of that date). William Mackenzie, second of Pitlundie and first of Culbo, was heir-male of his uncle George. His son George was his heir and successor, third of Pitlundie and second of Culbo, Sheriff-Substitute of Ross. His eldest son, William Mackenzie, M.D., of the H.E.I.C.S., became fourth of Pitlundie and third of Culbo. He died in 1866 and was succeeded in Culbo by his eldest surviving son, William Ord Mackenzie of Culbo, M.D., Deputy-Inspector-General of Army Hospitals, who became his father's heir.

The 1769 *"Plan of the estate and barony of Findon the property of Sir Roderick Mackenzie of Scatwell"* contains Wester Culbo and a vignette of Culbo House.

Two mounds were identified at Culbo, one at NH642610 possibly a field clearance heap, the other at NH646606 more possibly a chambered cairn.

Cullicudden Gaelic: *Cuil a'chudainn*

The Reverend Robert Arthur, minister of the United Parishes of Kirkmichael and Cullicudden, in 1792 was the first to suggest in print the origin of the name of Cullicudden: *"Couill-chuitin (contracted for Couill-chutigin), the Gaelic name of Cullicudden, signifies, the Nook, or Creek of Cuddies; a small delicate species of fish, well known on all the coasts of Scotland, which, during summer and beginning of harvest, are caught in great numbers along the shore of Cullicudden, particularly in a small creek a little above the old kirk."* This has been repeated by other sources uncritically ever since. Given a) the existence of the name for more than 500 years before Arthur, b) the feckleness of Cuddies (they had reportedly disappeared by the time of the NSA in 1836), and c) the inland presence and long-standing nature of the related *"Drumcudden,"* the origin would be worth revisiting by modern philologists. Nevertheless, the Cuddy origin is now a solid tradition in its own right.

Before Cullicudden Primary closed, a sculpture to commemorate it was erected in John Ross's field on the north side of the road beside the school. The sculpture, constructed out of ploughshares by Newhall Smithy to a design by pupils and art teacher Marian Tonkin, was based on the representation of the Cuddy on the school's badge.

Cullicudden – the settlement, Muir of Cullicudden and Bog of Cullicudden

Cullicudden is both the old parish and what has been called "*a scatter of houses beside the road,*" a community too disparate to be a hamlet but nevertheless with a long sense of individual identity.

The areas known as "*Bog of Cullicudden*" and "*Muir of Cullicudden*" are historically difficult to define precisely. Logically, the Muir would have applied to the drier moorground through which the modern Cullicudden Straight passes, and the Bog to the boggier areas down towards the burn. However, with some small areas of exception, the 1918 Newhall Estate Sale Particulars, in giving addresses for crofts, indicate that the Muir lay to the north and the Bog to the south of the Cullicudden Straight.

The Particulars give the Muir of Cullicudden as the location of crofts close to the road from the beginning of the estate (so the Muir would have extended further west) at Drumcudden Inn (Ellan Vannin) on the west to Alness Ferry Road on the east.

The Bog of Cullicudden in census returns and the 1918 Newhall Estate Sale Particulars is the area bounded by Springfield to the south, Easter St Martins to the west and the Church Road to the east (overlapping historically with the area also known as the Bog of Resolis). Somewhere within it was a bleaching-green, as the address of one of the 1843 Resolis rioters, David Mackenzie (dressed in a "*stripped sleeved vest and breeches with garters or leggings*") was "*Bleaching Green, Bog of Cullicudden.*"

Cullicudden School – see under Education.   NH64856393

Cullicudden Church (Listed) **and churchyard**   NH64976507

The church here was built, according to previous writers referring to the datestone above the remaining door, in 1609. However, it has been suggested that this part of the church may have been a later addition to an older building. Parts of the walls of what is is considered the south aisle are still standing, and the Kirkyard contains the tombs of most of the ministers in Resolis, together

with that of the Urquharts of Kinbeachie. In the gable, a moulded door and three panels (now empty) frame a window.

Two mounds of rubble represent the remainder of the church, although fragments of gravestone can also be seen amongst the rubble. RCAHMS reported what was considered the head of a 13th century double lancet window lying on one of the mounds of rubble, casting doubt, if this fragment had not been brought onto site from elsewhere, on the datestone representing the construction of the original church. Doubt is also raised by the presence of the earliest dated gravestone of 1600 and so many medieval carved stones of much earlier date. It would be useful for more detailed archaeological inspection to be carried out to establish a more robust historical basis for the site. Could this be the original parish church? Or was the earlier material moved from an earlier site, possibly from St Martins?

Set into the south wall, beside the gate, is a fine monument dated 1745 bearing the arms and initials of Master Thomas Inglis (minister of Resolis 1715-1747) and his wife Anne Urquhart. There is a 17th century burial enclosure of the Urquharts of Kinbeachie, balusters along top of its walls. Two heraldic stones are set in its east wall, one for Thomas Urquhart and one bearing date 1658 for John

The three boar heads of the Urquhart family, and the symbols of mortality: the deadbells, hourglass, gravedigger's tools and coffin.

Medieval cross with fleur-de-lis arising from a Calvary base, with axe and star on left and sword on right.

Urquhart and Isobel Cuthbert, his wife. There are other Urquhart of Kinbeachie stones outside the enclosure.

All easily accessed memorials have been transcribed by the author. As well as the stones bearing medieval crosses, some of the 18th and 19th century stones bear excellent assemblages of symbols of mortality and immortality. The oldest dated flatstone bears unusual features including three inverted toothed skulls arranged in a triangle, with the uppermost skull's teeth gnawing on the bone that stretches across the stone. The stone bears no names, only the date 1600.

The RCAHMS in the 1990s investigated medieval gravestones at Cullicudden and at other sites in the Moray Firth area (including Kirkmichael which also contains interesting examples). It is considered that Cullicudden is the largest and most impressive collection of monuments of its type. There are at least ten stones of 14th-16th century dates, and photographs of these are held at the National Monuments Record of Scotland at the RCAHMS and at Cromarty Courthouse; some are included in Alston and a simpler example is included here. These ornate stones are beautifully carved, bearing crosses with fleur-de-lis terminals running down the middle of the stone to meet a complex cross at the base, with often a sword running part of the length on one side.

These stones represent some of the finest artwork in Resolis and it is a pity that most lie unseen under the turf, although they are at least spared from erosion and damage caused by weather and man.

Cullicudden and Craigton – Cists (stone coffins)
At NH640641 and NH638639/NH638640 stone coffins were found in 1859, containing what were probably a cremation (the former) and an inhumation (the latter). In the 1970s, allegedly, the stones from a stone burial chamber or stone coffin, found on one of the farms in the area when land was being broken in, were quietly disposed of to avoid bother.

Cullicudden, Quarry   NH641644
There were several quarries along the Cullicudden shoreline, and the remnants of quays, from which boats carried the quarried stone, can still be detected beside at

Remains of pier at Cullicudden Quarry.

least two. The largest quarry lies north from Wester Cullicudden farmhouse.

Sage (1836) says: "*At Cullicudden, a freestone quarry has been opened, and in operation for many years. The materials of many public buildings and of stone piers have been taken from this quarry ... To secure the good materials which this quarry affords, the only way is to quarry at a considerable depth,– perhaps nine or twelve feet.*"

This quarry was rented from the Newhall Estate and over the years many families were associated with it, including three Urquhart brothers (involved in the 1843 Resolis Riot and delivering stone for the construction of Cromarty Free Church) and Alexander Munro. The bankruptcy proceedings of the latter in December 1862 give a useful indication of the activities of the quarry. He had taken the let of the Quarry about 1857 and spent at least £30 in working the quarry but it was not a paying concern. He took a contract in 1861 for a railway cutting at Grantown, but a partner in the contract, Peter Boyle, took up about £62 of their money and left the country leaving Munro to meet the men's wages himself, which he did by selling a crane for £18 which had cost £26. He lost about £30 through the wreck "*in July last*" of a lighter used in carrying stones from the quarry. His debtors included Donald Corbett Quarrier Cullicudden, James Forbes, Donald Dingwall and William Macdonald, all quarrymen at Cullicudden, and a range of other Cullicudden workmen.

When much of the Newhall Estate was put up for sale in 1918, the Cullicudden Quarry was reserved, but it has never operated since.

Wester Cullicudden Farm, **Easter Cullicudden Farm**   NH642642, NH655652
Two long-established farmsteads a mile apart. At Wester Cullicudden (for many years in the 19th and 20th centuries farmed by the Macivers, previously in Templand, Avoch), a track was once in regular use but is at present partly blocked, running eastward to the Dell Farmhouse and along past Cullicudden Croft to Easter Cullicudden. From Wester Cullicudden, with a dogleg up to the Craigton road, this route once ran right through to Shoretown, joining all the farmsteads that lie halfway between the top of the Cullicudden ridge and the sea.

At Easter Cullicudden, associated for several generations with the influential Macfarquhar family, there was a waterwheel which powered a bruiser. A piggery here was built from the stones of the ruined steading at Wester Alness Ferry. The Macfarquhars took a keen interest in the local school. John Macfarquhar, who died in 1955 aged 85, owned the first car in the area in the early 1900s.

The roads then were clay and stones. Stone breaking was a regular job, with several lay-bys where stones were deposited for stonebreakers to work their way through. One such location was at the top of Mill Road (now North View), where in the 1930s an old man lived in a caravan and earned his living breaking stones. Then, replacing the stonebreakers, came a big machine simply known as "*the Crusher*" based in the rough ground at "*Danses*" (see the Dell).

The Dell Farmhouse, Cullicudden Croft   NH64846438, NH65176447
A tenancy within Wester Cullicudden, the farm which became known as the Dell was occupied by the Scott family for a period in the 19th-20th centuries. A Sundial is shown here in 1880 and 1905. East of the Dell is a crofthouse once occupied by Urquharts in the mid 1800s, and now known as Cullicudden Croft; the original foundation stones are still visible at the base of its walls.

The road down to the farmhouse is known as Dell Road. Across the main road from Dell Road used to lie an area of heather, above the ruin at NH653638 once known as "*Danses*" (named after "*Dan*" Fowler and brother Alec who lived there). In the 1930s, Hercher's Sideshows would take camp on this heath and stay for two or three nights entertaining the local folk.

The Den   NH688642
The drift geology of the Den caused Angus Beaton in 1894 to wax lyrical: "*There is yet another remarkable deposit of diluvial clay at Allt Dubhach and Newhall Burn which deserves notice. The best route to reach 'The Den,' as it is also called, is to drive or walk along the Shore Road from Cromarty and past Jemimaville, until you reach the point where the stream pours its waters into Udale Bay; proceed up the side of the burn until you leave Braelangwell House a little behind; now you catch glimpses of the red clay cliffs between openings in the thick foliage, for here are the bright wavy leaves of the silver birch; the outstretched branches of the oak, the spruce, the larch, and the dark pine, the shivering poplar and the gigantic elm; while the banks are carpeted with soft, springy moss, the yellow primrose, and the bonnie bracken. The stillness of this quiet retreat is broken by the soothing ripple of the brook; the hushed rustling of the leaves; the rich notes of the mavis, and the sweet melody of a hundred feathered choristers... The chief difference between the clay deposit here and that in Rosemarkie Glen is, that, while in the latter comparatively few boulders are embedded in the matrix, here we find ice-scratched and rounded boulders, polished to a very high degree, lying about in all directions; while some of the escarpments present the appearance of a pudding stone. Polished boulders of granite and whinstone, weighing many tons, half protrude themselves in the face of the clay, others reveal only a rounded shoulder, while many seem tottering on the brink of the bank, as if 'An infant hand might urge Their headlong passage down the verge.'*"

Drumcudden   NH642632 (general area)
Gaelic *Druimchudainn*. *Druim* is a ridge and for *cudden* see Cullicudden. Variants: Dromcudyn 1328; Drumcudyn 1528 and 1546; Drumcudden 1458.
The lands of Drumcudden, as owned by the Duff family, are clearly set out in the estate plan of 1796 "*Lands of Drumcudden Property of Captain Hugh Robert Duff of Muirton.*" Much of the land formerly associated with Drumcudden is

now termed St Martins, which previously was of more limited extent. Indeed, the present St Martins steading was once the yard of Easter Drum-Cuddin. The rectangular tiny estate stretched from the west end of the Cullicudden Straight, south to the burn, along the burn to St Martins Mill, north past Ellan Vannin (the Drumcudden Inn) across the main road a short distance and then back to the west end of the Cullicudden Straight.

In 1328 King Robert Bruce settled a controversy between Hugh Earl of Ross and Sir Andrew de Moravia about the lands of Dromcudyn and Munlochy. In 1458, Drumcudden was leased to Alexander Flemyng of Ross from King James II. The town of Drumnecudyne is, about 1561, enumerated among the lands of the parish. In 1586 King James VI granted in heritage to William Keith the master of his wardrobe the lands of Drumquhidden, for the yearly payment of £6. 13s. 4d., 2 chalders 6 bolls 1 firlot of bear, 4 bolls of oats, 1 mart, 1 mutton, 48 poultry, 20 s. of bondage silver, 10 reek hens and 80 loads of fuel. In 1666 John Monro of Ardulzie was served heir to his father Hugh Monro of Ardulzie in the davach of the town and lands of Drumcuddin in the barony of Delnie, lordship of Ardmeanach, and sheriffdom of Ross.

Drumcudden came into the hands of the Duffs of Drummuir and Muirtown (Inverness) near the end of the 17th century, and they held onto it for more than a century.

There is a Crown Charter dated 8 June 1681 in favour of William Duff, chamberlain of the earldom of Ross, of the lands of Drumcudden with the privilege of an alehouse. Many Instruments of Sasine subsequently record the passing on of Drumcudden from William (who became provost of Inverness) through Duff descendants. In 1801, the Lands of Drumcudden were held by Hugh Robert Duff of Muirtown Esqr.

The 1796 estate plan contains many additional features of interest other than the boundary of the estate. As usual, the estate is seen to consist of areas of cultivated land surrounded by common moorland (*e.g.* "*Undivided Moor Ground possessed in common betwixt the tennants of Drumcuddin* [and] *those of Cullycuddin.*") Two roads run along the north west: the "*Old Road from Dingwall to Inverbreaky and Cromarty*" forms the undulating boundary of Drumcudden, and present-day, dead straight "*New Road from Dingwall to Inverbreaky and Cromarty*" (with its angled turn at the south west end) lies partially in Drumcudden. The new straight road, down which cars now race at illegal and ever-increasing speeds, was thus just replacing the previous tortuous route.

A third road described as "*Road from Kinbeaky to the Church of Cully Cuddin*" runs through Drumcudden south to north, incorporating the present St Martins footpath. It demonstrates the importance of the Church as a destination.

In 1836, Drumcudden is described as a small property lately improved, and at present in the hands of the Trustees of the late Donald McKenzie, Esq. of

Newhall, consisting principally of church lands, and paying a heavy rent to the Crown.

Drumcudden exists now only as a house on the Craigton road at Wester Cullicudden, named by teacher and local history enthusiast, the late Penny Poole.

Drumcudden Inn (Ellan Vannin)   NH64536380

The lands of Drumcudden were always described as being "*with the privilege of an alehouse.*"

As usual, there are criminal records associated with incidents at the inn. In another "*cross-county*" case, in 1852, John Simpson, farm servant, Brae, was accused at Cromarty Sheriff Court of assault on Donald Macrae, farmer and inn-keeper, Drumcudden, and Hector Macrae, shopkeeper. Alexander MacKintosh, farmer, Brae, agreed to stand bail of two hundred merks, Scots. The case was deserted because the assault occurred in Ross-shire. However, Simpson appears to have been later fined 1 guinea for his assault on Donald Macrae.

In 1918, the licence for the Drumcudden Inn was bought out from the Innkeeper, Donald Urquhart, and extinguished by the Central Control Board (Liquor Traffic), in an attempt to control the sale of alcohol around the Cromarty Firth.

The report to the Board of 26 February 1918 is of interest: "*I paid a visit to Drumcudden Inn yesterday, the 25th inst. The house is on the main Dingwall road about 4 miles to the west of Balblair Ferry and almost directly opposite Alness. The house has quite a good appearance and the accommodation much about the same as Balblair Inn. On ground floor there is Dining-room, Sitting-room, Bar with cellar underneath, Kitchen and Scullery, on the whole a decent little property, and I believe would be assessed at about £500. Urquhart, the*

Ellan Vannin, the former Drumcudden Inn.

proprietor, gave me to understand his turnover in spirits was about 350 proof galls., very little beer sold. There is a small farm of 20 acres belonging to the house, also a small general store which Urquhart looks after. I can quite well see the trade is principally a passing one and I think could be well done without, Balblair being all that is necessary. In asking my opinion I should say do away with the license, allowing the man to remain in his house and farm, as he will be quite pleased to do. / (sgd). J.C. Chisholm / P.S. There are five bed-rooms, box room and lavatory upstairs."

The Inn continued for some years without a licence, the last "*hotelkeeper*" noted (in the Valuation Roll of 1924/5) being Donald Macleod. Apparently there was a well in the cellar of the east room of the Inn, very handy for the housekeeper. Marriages there were common – for example, three out of the seven marriages in Resolis in 1909 took place at "*the Drumcudden Hotel.*" The road beside the Inn descended to the shore. When a coal boat came in, locals went down this road with horse and cart to collect their supply.

Walker states that Ellan Vannin is Manx for "*the Black Isle,*" but it is actually Manx for "*the Isle of Man.*" The Inn had temporarily become Drynoch House. W.G. Mackenzie (father of the well-known "*D.U.*" (Donald Urquhart) Mackenzie), was originally from Ferintosh, owned shops in Liverpool, and lived in Drumdyre. When the Mackenzies moved into the old Inn, around 1939/40, it was renamed Ellan Vannin as W.G.'s wife was from the Isle of Man. For many years now, it has been rented accommodation.

Drumdyre   NH648622 (general area)
Gaelic: *Druim*, a ridge, doubtfully *Druim(a)doighr*, (*Daighre* was an Irish personal name).
Farmsteads have existed at Drumdyre for a long time, but with few records. The first reference I have found is in the marriage on 18 July 1766 between "*Alexander Munro tacksman in Drumdyre & Janet Munro daughter to Finla Munro tacksman in Toberchurn.*" The first edition of the Ordnance Survey (1870s) shows a farmstead at NH647626 (Easter Drumdyre) and NH647621 (Wester Drumdyre).

The memory of one long-lived tenant in Drumdyre was used in two civil cases.

The first was in 1816 when evidence for the break-up of the Mulbuie Commonty was being considered: "*Compeared Donald Simpson, tenant in Drumdyre of Newhall, aged 74 years, who being solemnly sworn, &c. depones, That he has known the lands of Easter Culbo for forty-three years bygone. And depones, and concurs with the preceding witness as to the fact of the muir ground above this house being a common, and of the tenants of Easter Culbo frequenting the Milbuy without interruption.*"

The second was in 1822 in a boundary dispute: "*Compeared John Urquhart Esq late of Kinbeachie aged Seventy years and upwards, a Witness called on the part of Mr Sheppard, who being Solemnly Sworn and Examined, purged of malice and partial Counsel, Depones That he was born in Kinbeachie in this neighbourhood, and resided in this parish chiefly for the last Twenty five years, and that he has frequently been informed, that Aultnamiel is the March between the Counties of Ross and Cromarty, that in particular, the Deponent was informed of this by the Deceased Donald Simpson sometime tenant in Drumdyre who was an Old Man at the time he gave him the information."*

Elder Cottage   NH663646
The first record of this name (of a recently-demolished cottage at Bog of Cullicudden) found is in the 1927/8 Valuation Roll. An elder tree still stands beside the ruin.

Ellan Vannin – see Drumcudden Inn.

Ellenslea   NH70306496
The former United Free Church manse, situated at the lower entrance to Braelangwell. Aerial photography indicates archaeological interest close to Ellenslea in the form of a Barrow and Cultivation Remains at NH706649.

Fanny's Brae
The steep hill from the B9163 down to Resolis Memorial Hall, passing the east entrance to the Church of Scotland. Walker states it was named after an old lady who lived at the top of the hill. It is not clear in which house (if it still exists) the lady called Fanny lived. Walker states that in the past congregations attending at Communion Seasons were so large that services were held out of doors, and the Sacrament Spot can still be seen *"at the East end of the glebe on Fanny's Brae."*
     Surprisingly rarely seen in records, apart from Walker's 1958 Booklet, although from personal experience in common usage 1950s to now. The Valuation Rolls contain the address of a lady through the 1960s as *"Woodside, Fanny's Brae, Balblair."*

Fern Cottage   NH65636451
(Fearn Cottage on 1901 Census; *Fearn* is Gaelic for the elder tree)
One of many botanically-named residences on the Cullicudden Straight. This was, at the end of the 19th and beginning of the 20th centuries the site of a smiddy operated by a MacGregor family. Temporarily known as **Craig Isle**, but now again known as Fern Cottage.

Ferryton   NH683663 (general area)
A common earlier variant is Ferrytown. The origin of the name is self-evident, although the precise ferry to which it refers is unclear. The earliest references

include 1623 (Privy Council Register), *c*1637 (Gordon map), 1654 (Blaeu map).

Like many other parts of Resolis, it is hard to visualise from the few farmhouses and steadings presently in the Ferryton area the density of population in the past. There were 27 households given as Ferryton in 1851; many houses have since simply disappeared into the turf.

Ferryton Point projects well into the Firth. A Cairn and Post are shown at Low Water Mark at the Point in the 1898 Admiralty Chart. A 1999 RCAHMS report states that 1995 oblique aerial photography has revealed the crop-mark of a ring-ditch, measuring about 10 m in diameter, 100 m west south west of Ferryton Storehouse. There are also records of cairns which formerly existed at Easter Ferryton, Mid Ferryton and Wester Ferryton, now removed.

Ferryton Point – Girnal (Storehouse)   NH68016696
Industrial Monument Listed
This long, two-storeyed late 18th century warehouse, standing close to the beach at Ferryton Point, was subject to a residential conversion in 1990. The Scottish Vernacular Buildings Working Group 1989 Conference Proceedings contain drawings of the building before its conversion. The walls were made of sandstone rubble, sea-washed boulders and lime mortar, with dressed sandstone margins. It had one door on the north and three on the south, and there was a stair outside the west gable to reach the upper floor. Little is known of the physical shipping arrangements from the girnal although the curved shingle beach at Ferryton Point would allow boats to be easily drawn up. Alston states it was originally built as a single-storey building and later heightened, the external stairs added to access the first floor.

Known locally simply as *"The Storehouse,"* it is the end of many shoreline walks as it lies at the foot of one of the few tracks with beach access. The building was originally the Newhall Girnal, the estate storehouse where rents in kind, such as grain or meal, were received from tenants, stored and in due course exported by sea. In 1773, the laird of Newhall, William Gordon, wrote of having spent two days here *"morning to night, accounting with my tenants, without any assistant, writing, figuring, entering in Compts Books ... and now half crazed and half asleep."* The office was located in the west end of the ground floor.

In 1843, Newhall allowed its use as a preaching station by Donald Sage and his congregation who had come out from the parish church in the Disruption. They utilised the upper storey but it was apparently so dark and uncomfortable (and the congregation so large) that they used it only in inclement weather when it was impossible to worship in the open air.

The Firichean
Gaelic: *Fireach*, plural *Firichean*, a Gaelic term rarely used nowadays meaning moor, moorland, hill land. The 1769 Drumcudden Estate map shows moor

ground on both sides of the road at the high end of the Cullicudden Straight.

Walker states that Firichean, meaning "*the moors,*" refers to the open country divided in two by the main road, immediately west of St Martins. However, it does appear to be applied to the road itself, the west end of the Cullicudden Straight, that three mile stretch of straight B9163 that commences after the bend at the Drumdyre junction and terminates just before the Corrie. Many a late-night traveller "*coming down the Firichean*" has drifted off to sleep and drifted onto the adjacent fields.

The name is rarely heard now, but lives on in the parish in the name of Firichean House, the home of the author.

Fleucherries

Gaelic: *Fliuchairidh*, the wet place; a locative of *fliuch-ar-adh*, from *fliuch*, wet. First record noted in 1819 in the evidence given in the Division of the Commonty, where it is stated to be the source of the "*Auduig*" (Allt Dubhach), to the west of the crofts of Agnes Hill. Populated, as in use in 1841 with "*John Elder Fleuchary*" on the Poors Roll and on the Valuation Roll, *e.g.* 1900/1.

Fraoch or Froach Cottage   NH66126481

Gaelic: *Fraoch* heather. Another housename of botanical origin. Name first noted: 1901 Census. Fraoch Cottage was long associated with the Cameron family, Roderick John, who was a master shoemaker, and his children. One of those children was known locally as "*the Dom*" (for Dominie or teacher), William Cameron (1874-1933), schoolmaster at Petty and a great Gaelic singer.

Gordon's Mill – Planned Village   NH706654

Named after Henrietta Gordon of Newhall (see Newhall) who was noted for improving the estate, it has been recorded as Gordonsmill, Gordon's Mills and variants thereof. The first reference found to the name is on 13 March 1811 in the baptism of Jannet, daughter of James Urquhart wright Gordon's Mills & Cathrine Hendry, but it would have been in existence for some years prior to this.

The listed mill building at Gordon's Mill was built in 1796 (the date on a skewstone) as a carding and spinning mill. Additional plots were established in a line on either side of the mill to initiate a new settlement, and Alston states there was a waulk or fulling mill nearby. The enterprise failed in 1815.

John McLeod Esquire bought Gordon's Mill for £1,040 in 1819 following this advertisement by Donald Mackenzie of Newhall in the Inverness Journal: "*The Lands and Village of GORDONSMILL, with the Mill and Feus thereof, as possessed by sundry Tenants. There is a valuable Machinery belonging to the Proprietor attached to the Mill. This Property lies upon the Cromarty Frith, has abundance of water, is surrounded by good Roads, and is well suited for carrying on Trade.*"

McLeod had an unhappy time in Gordon's Mill. In 1831, his blood boiled over and he produced a list of grievances against Newhall for redress: he has not received an acre of land to which he is entitled, and which is still being cropped by a neighbouring farmer, John Simson, one of Newhall's tenants; Simson has shut up one of his mill lades; he has been obliged to make up a mill dam himself or lose the benefit of the woollen mill; Simson is now complaining that this mill dam is injuring his crop on the land which Simson should not be cropping anyway; Simson has dared to cut a hole in McLeod's boundary dyke; Newhall's Mr Kelly has rooted out trees planted by McLeod himself in his own land well within his boundary of the Burn of Camalty; an earthen dyke within his boundary has been cut away by Hector Holm Farmer to the north of it to put on his land so the dyke is now in a tottering state; and he has never been given possession of the strip of land to the south of Gordonmill to which he is entitled. McLeod winds up this list of grievances by bringing up an issue affecting his social status, clearly the hardest to thole. He pays more in proportion than any other Proprietor in the Parish for Kirk dues, yet he has never been given the right to his own personal Seat, and as for his Servants, "*they are obliged to wander through the Church and sit where they can get a Seat, which is hard when their Master is a Proprietor in the Parish.*"

Unlike the other planned village in Resolis, Jemimaville, Gordon's Mill did not take off. In 1836, the population of the Village of Gordon's Mill was only 42. Indeed, the location and number of buildings in the 1819 plan of the village is little changed even now.

A serious charge is found in the Kirk Session Records for 7 March 1831, involving Anne Cameron alias McKiddy at Gordons Mills. She had been delated for a Dilapse in Fornication, on the clear evidence of her having had a child. The Session had been unimpressed with her declaration "*that the Father of her child was a Man she met on the high road returning from Inverness to whom she was an utter stranger & whom she neither knew nor asked his name or place of residence.*"

The Session were convinced that this was "*nothing else but a wicked pretence on the part of said Anne Cameron to conceal the real Father of her illegitimate offspring,– and that she evidently appears to be bribed by him to conceal by this highly improbable story his name & designation... Considering further that said Anne Cameron is well known to have concealed her pregnancy untill the very time of her delivery thereby rendering it very suspicious, at least, that she intended in a very criminal manner to conceal her guilt altogether,– that at all times her general character, has been very loose & profligate & that she is also guilty of contumacy,*" the Session declared the poor woman "*to be under the Sentence of the lesser Excommunication to be cut off from all outward privileges.*"

Gordon's Mill – Watermill Listed   NH70646541

Built in 1796 (the date on a skewstone), Gordon's Mill was in operation from January 1797, under a manager and others brought in who had a knowledge of "*sorting, scribbling, carding and spinning.*" The owner expressed the hope that the mill would provide employment and "*meliorate the condition of the people, many of whom are yearly emigrating to other countries.*" However, following the failure of the wool carding exercise in 1815, the mill was converted to grind grain.

In the late 20th century it was simply used as an agricultural shed, when it was described thus: "*It is a rectangular two-storey and attic, four-bay rubble building with ashlar facing at the wheel gable. The wheel and machinery have been removed but marks on the gable indicate that there have been at least three wheels on the site, two about 12ft (3.66m) diameter, one about 14ft (4.27m); the last was about 4ft 6in (1.37m) wide.*"

It was subject to a sympathetic residential conversion in two phases in 1991 and 1997. The wheel marks on the gable, the 1796-dated skewstone on the east gable and many original features are still on display.

The converted Gordon's Mill.

Waterwheel marks on the east
wall above the water race,
demonstrating at least three
different wheels in the mill's history.

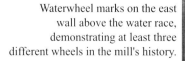

Hamewith Name of recent origin   NH69476506

Henrietta Wood and Henrietta Park   NH686656
Like Gordon's Mill, named after Henrietta Gordon of Newhall. Ash states that
Henrietta was an enthusiastic planter, and that the farm of Henrietta Park began
as a plantation named for her. The planting of Henrietta Wood and the
subsequent building of the farm square and Gordon's Mill are documented in a
series of estate plans at Newhall House.
   Alston draws attention to a good example of an early stone dyke at Henrietta
Park, dating to the 1770s, adding that the earliest stone dykes had a very broad
section and looked, in cross-section, more like a mound of loosely piled stones.
They were often built up with earth on one side, intended only to keep cattle out
of areas planted with trees.

Hillcrest Name of recent origin.   NH69086627

Inch   NH673664 (Inch farmhouse)
Gaelic: *Inis* island or wet meadowland.
On 24 July 1666, a sasine, dated 9 July 1666, was registered in favour of Hugh
Dallas, Commissary Clerk of Ross, for himself, Christian Lauder, his spouse, and
William Dallas, their eldest son, by James Dallas of Balblair as bailie,
constituted by a contract of excambion made between Sir John Urquhart of
Cromarty with consent of Dame Barbara Mackenzie, his spouse, and Hugh
Dallas, his wife and son, dated 6th June last, whereby they acquired the lands of
Ferritoune, Auchmartine, and Inches; and they were accordingly infeft in these
lands.
   The farm now known as Inch is reached by a western branch off the road to
Ferryton Point. However, once a track ran from Easter Alness Ferry through Inch
to Ferryton. In the first half of the 20th century, sheep were driven along this
track from neighbouring farms to the dipping facilities at Inch.

Inch – Cnoc nan Taibhsean – Cairn Scheduled   NH67166609
Gaelic: Hill of the Ghosts. An unchambered round cairn described thus: *"This
disturbed cairn stands 400m SW of Inch farmhouse; it measures 8.5m in
diameter and 0.6m in height."*

Inch – Cairns
Two further cairns at NH677665 and NH672661, close to Inch farmhouse, are
reported as destroyed by cultivation.

Inch – Loch Buidhe (Gaelic: Yellow Loch) **and Loch Inch**
Loch Buidhe was a small loch (now drained) on the moor to the west of the road

down to Inch farmhouse. Loch Inch was a much more extensive, though still shallow, loch, partly dry in summer. Frequented by great numbers of nesting gulls, these moorland lochs used to draw local children who would raid the nests for eggs.

Inverbreakie – see Balblair.

Ivy Cottage   NH66286491
Another botanical name, Ivy Cottage was occupied for a long time in the 1900s by Murrays, an old Resolis family. There was a carpenter's workshop here, and an undertaker's business.

To the west of the drive going in to Ivy Cottage was the carpenter's workshop, with circular saw and an engine that could be difficult to start. The coffins were made in the lean-to at the west end. At night, eight men would carry the coffin from the lean-to to the appropriate house, taking turns four about. Hugh Murray and a helper would put the body in the coffin, and everyone would have a whisky at the wyke.

One night my father was helping to carry the coffin along the road when, out of the darkness, came a man on a bike without lights on. He ran into the coffin, and was greatly shaken. My father was at the front with another chap, and the cyclist, a ploughman from Resolis, who was on a racing bike and hence had his head down, went between the pair of them and was badly winded. My father reported prosaically that the ploughman had to sit down for a while but he did not damage the coffin.

Jemimaville
Named after Jamima Charlotte Graham, who in 1822 married Sir George Gun Munro of Poyntzfield and whose money enabled its establishment. All sorts of dates of origin are given by different sources but the Kirk Session records of 1831 state that it was created in 1822. References in the late 1820s and early 1830s give it as Jamima Village, Jamimaville, Jamemaville and variants thereof, before it settled down to its present name.

Some sources conflated the wives of the first (Sir George Gun Munro, wife Mary Hinde ms Poyntz) and the fourth (George Gun Munro, wife Jamima Charlotte Graham) Lairds of Poyntzfield into a fictional heiress called Jemima Poyntz whose money allowed Munro to establish Jemimaville and in whose honour the estate of Ardoch was renamed Poyntzfield. The story is now deeply embedded in the folklore of the parish.

Another story links Jemimaville and Barbaraville (on the opposite side of the Firth), in that Jemima and Barbara were sisters and their husbands, when establishing the two villages in these locations facing each other, were commemorating the sisters' affection (one version) or rivalry (another version). I have closely examined the family of Jamima Graham, who was of the family of Graham of Drynie, and the origins of Barbaraville, which seems likely to have been initiated by Kenneth McLeay of Newmore, and whose mother, sister and daughter were all called Barbara, but have not yet identified a link between the two.

Jemimaville is one-sided, with practically all its buildings quaintly on the north side of the road. The water supply initially was from two pumps (see the section on Angus Munro) on the south side of the road requiring negotiation of any traffic; the two iron pumps can still be seen. The current Post Office, a tiny wooden structure, is one of the few buildings to the south of the road, sitting incongruously in a field. The Post Office in Jemimaville was previously situated in the substantial sandstone building in the west end of the village and closed in 1989.

Whilst there are a few buildings closer to the Firth, the impression of the village is, as created, of one row of earlier nineteenth century, terraced, single storey cottages set along the road. Many of the cottages have ornate skew-putts, projecting, rolled, scrolled or with "*club skews with rope mouldings for decoration.*" The houses are of sandstone, and box-dormers were added to several in the 20th century. The door lintel of "*Burnside,*" the first house from the east, bears the date 1826. One fine two storey building bears two inset panels between the three second storey windows. The west panel contains a shield bearing the symbols of a tailor, from top: tailor's goose, scissors, pressing board,

the east a shield bearing date 1879.

Advertisements appeared in the 1820s and 1830s promoting the development of Jemimaville, for example (1826): "*FEUS in JAMEMAVILLE on very advantageous terms; also very profitable situations for Tailors and Shoemakers, who can command a little Capital, where, by letter, (post paid) or on application to Major Munro, at Poyntzfield House, by Cromarty, further particulars will be known*" and (1833) "*NOTICE. NEW MARKETS AT JAMIMA VILLAGE, POYNTZFIELD, CROMARTYSHIRE. At the suggestion of the Farmers, and Inhabitants of the District, Major Munro has resolved to establish Three MARKETS, for the Sale of Horses, Cattle (Pigs in particular), Farm and every other kind of Produce.*"

Munro even developed a ship building yard. In 1841: "*LAUNCH.– On Thursday, the 25th instant, a beautiful and well-built barque of 80 tons O.M., belonging to Mr George Morrison, was launched from the building yard at Jemima-ville, on Major Munro's estate of Poyntzfield. The sight throughout was pleasant and amusing. The day being fine added to the enjoyment, and induced many spectators to assemble from the neighbouring towns and district of country around... as soon as she began to move, immediately before entering the water, the ceremony of naming was gone through, by Mrs Munro of Poyntzfield, to whom the honour of name was presented, which was performed by taking a bottle of wine in her hand, and breaking it on the bowsprit, saying, 'I name thee Jemima.'* ... *This vessel, we understand, is built altogether of the wood taken*

Above: original Free Church Manse, Jemimaville.
Right, above: shield bearing symbols of a tailor.
Right, below: ornate skewputt.
Opposing page: sandstone frontage of Jemimaville.

from the Poyntzfield estate. ... From the great facilities which the building yard affords, as also from the abundance of wood in the neighbourhood, we hope to see many others launched from the same spot with equal safety and success."

By 1836, the population of Jemimaville had grown to 147, and the lists of occupations of residents show a diverse range of artisans.

The first Free Church (at NH71966526) was completed in 1844 – see section on Organised Religion. The first Free Church Manse was also completed c1844. It is much more spacious than it appears from the road as it continues down for another floor. It stands out from its neighbours with twin bowed outer bays linked above the main door by a continuous piended roof which is supported by two columns. The former Church of Scotland Mission (at NH71706511) at the west end of the village was used as a Public Hall, but is not at present in use.

The Resolis boundary in Jemimaville ends at the bridge over the burn. The south parapet of the bridge bears the carved date 1800. Just east of this is the gateway to Udale on the south side of the road and Scott's garage on the north side. The curiously shaped garage (NH72156521) was, in fact, previously the United Free church, erected in 1906 just to the west of Newmills, and re-erected at this location, just outside the parish. Scott's garage commenced in Jemimaville with a petrol pump in the square.

Trouble at the Inn, Jemimaville

A village, of course, had to have an Inn, and the one in Jemimaville seemed to draw every kind of trouble.

It wasn't long before the innkeeper attracted the attention of the Kirk Session. In 1824, Elder James Thomson *"reported that he had been credibly informed that a Raffle was to be held at the House of Alexander Munro Vintner in Jemimaville. The Session considering that Raffles being a species of gambling are not only illegal but if tolerated as a practice would be very pernicious to the Morals of the People feel it to be their duty to use their authority & best endeavours to put a stop to it. The Moderator was appointed to send a writ in intimation by the officer to the said Alexander Munro cautioning him against the consequences of holding such an illegal meeting in his house & in case of his refusal, intimating that the Session would prosecute him before a civil Magistrate."*

In 1832, Alexander Munro, Vinter at Jemimaville, was again in trouble for sabbath profanation. One Saturday a party had been drinking in Munro's Inn, had moved on to the house of Alexander McLeay in the village where they were drinking whisky until after midnight, whisky having been sent for from Munro's, in consequence of which one man *"was lying drunk in a house in the village untill his wife came for him at three o clock of that day."* Munro was reprimanded by the Kirk Session.

In 1840, Hugh Bethune, tailor, Jemimaville, was fined for assaulting William

MacKenzie near what was now the inn of Walter Ross. In the same year, William Paterson and Colin Mackenzie were accused of breaking into the inn, assaulting Walter Ross and Janet Junor, his wife, and pulling down the inn sign.

In 1841, there was a series of court cases initiated by the forced sale at the Smithy of the implements of Hugh Sinclair, Blacksmith in Jemimaville. His wife, Christian MacDonald, threw stones at John Rose, hardware merchant Invergordon, at Jemimaville. With other women, she attacked the men who had come with carts to remove the goods sold to pay Sinclair's creditor. She assaulted James Munro carter Invergordon with a stick in the inn of Walter Ross.

Some of the blacksmith tools that had been poinded were sold to Major Munro of Poyntzfield for the use of the new blacksmith. The enterprising Hugh was some time after accused of forcing an entry to the smithy, Poyntzfield, and stealing his own tools back. He had left Jemimaville, and was resident at Culloden, but was now a prisoner in the Tollbooth of Cromarty.

Poor Hugh had a hard time of it. Alexander MacKenzie, Merchant, Cromarty, even poinded his 24 drills of potatoes, valued at £3.12.0, on a field belonging to Major Munro.

In 1843, Peter Angus, Second Mate of the Atlanta Revenue Cutter, and seven other men, called at the Inn of Walter Ross, Jemimaville. They unwisely left some articles in a cellar under lock and key for safe-keeping – a copper-bottomed bailer and a fermenting tin used for distillation. In Ross's absence his house was entered and articles stolen.

In 1847, several men were even fined for a riot in the inn at Jemimaville belonging to Walter Ross, the Innkeeper.

A long peaceful period ensued – until the time of James Ballantyne as Innkeeper. The name of the Inn at this time was the Plough, and was described in the 1870s as: "*Plough Inn. This name applies to a small one storey thatched Inn with the usual Village accommodation. It is situated about the centre of the Village.*" Ballantyne was a very different man to Walter Ross for, as often as not, this Innkeeper was assaulting rather than being assaulted. At first he seems to be on the receiving side. In 1869, the case of Duncan Cruickshank assaulting James Ballantyne, Innkeeper at Jemimaville, was found not proven, but, in 1873, David Ross and Donald Ross, farm servants, Allerton, were fined £3 each for assaulting James Ballantyne in his Inn and then attacking Donald Junner, Police Constable in the execution of his duty, Kenneth MacKay, miller at Poyntzfield and Hector Finlayson, Farm Servant at Ardiville. However, Ballantyne began to go on the offence, for in 1875 there is a record of James Ballantyne "*innkeeper, Plough Inn, Jemimaville*" being fined 30s for assaulting Malcolm Fraser, lodging at the inn, by seizing him by the whiskers and dragging him along the floor, and into the bargain even assaulting his own wife Barbara Campbell or Ballantyne.

Ballantyne gave up the Inn about 1877, but did not give up his wild ways. In 1877, he was found guilty of assault, having used threatening behaviour to

Alexander Mackay and broken a chair in the inn at Jemimaville. He was expelled, returned and assaulted Mackay. Again, in 1878, he was found guilty of attacking Simon Fraser on the road leading to Inverbreakie Ferry.

Peace appears to have descended with Ballantyne's departure, as there was an extended period before the next case of assault, in 1886, when James Thom, tailor, Jemimaville, assaulted Thomas Ross, PC, at what was now being called *"the Poyntzfield Arms Inn,"* occupied by James Grant McKay. In 1897, Charles Matheson, stonebreaker, Jemimaville assaulted Andrew MacKenzie, carpenter, Agnes Hill, in James Gray's Inn, Jemimaville. In 1901, the County Sanitary Inspector fined Mrs Williamina Morrison Thom or Gray, wife of the innkeeper of the Poyntzfield Arms Inn, having purchased whisky within the Inn from Mrs. Gray considered not up to standard.

Like the Drumcudden Inn, in 1918 the licence was bought out and extinguished as part of the liquor control measures around the Firth. The former Poyntzfield Arms Inn is the two-storey building in the square now known as Bay View, two doors west from Barnacle Cottage. It is understood that the iron ring outside is that to which horses were once tethered.

The Battle of Jemimaville

On 26th October 1914 a coastguard on patrol at the mouth of the Cromarty Firth reported a submarine sneaking into the firth past the then-incomplete boom. There appears to have been naval paranoia about submarines at this time. When an object was subsequently seen moving up the south side of the firth, HMS Queen Mary and HMS Lion began shelling. Firing was wild and inaccurate, and there were ricochets, the result being that shells passed into and over Jemimaville, and into the woods and hillsides opposite.

Several houses had their roofs holed. A four-inch shell passed clean through one roof, scattering slates, penetrating walls, detonating on the road and breaking every window in the vicinity. In this house a baby, Alexandrina McGill, was seriously injured, but amazingly there were no fatalities.

The incident caused great excitement locally, and the story grew in the telling (the Inverness Courier in its Stop Press column that evening reported that two submarines had been sunk), but Admiralty and Navy embarrassment led to a suppression of the incident.

Jemimaville – mound; urn   *c*NH7265

Sage reported in 1836: *"An earthen tumulus or mound being broken into at Jemimaville by Major Munro of Poyntzfield to procure gravel for metalling a road, an earthen urn of a very antique form was found in it, and which is at present in the possession of that gentleman."* More recent efforts to identify the precise location of this site have been unsuccessful.

Kempfield   NH64886398
House immediately to east of Cullicudden School built by long-serving (1878-
1900s) Cullicudden schoolmaster Kenneth Kemp on his retiral. Name first noted
in 1924/5 Valuation Roll.

Kinbeachie   NH630620 (general area)
Gaelic: *Cinn a'bheathchaidh*, head of the birch wood (*beithach*). Variants
Kynbarch 1561-66, Kinbeachie 1565-71.
Kinbeachie was the estate in Resolis that was retained in the Urquhart name for
the longest time, up to 1893, although the route of inheritance was exceedingly
complex.
   Kinbeachie came into the Urquhart family in 1585 by means of a Charter
from the Bishop of Ross. Sir Thomas Urquhart inherited it from Walter, his
grandfather, and exchanged it in 1611 with Thomas Urquhart of Davidston (near
Cromarty), who married a Margaret Monro of Coul and was succeeded by his
two sons Walter and Thomas. In the Kinbeachie enclosure in Kirkmichael there
are to be found stones with the younger Thomas's Armorial Bearings and those
of both his first wife, Janet Williamson, and his second wife, Agnes Munro
(*"Heir lie ane honest / woman called AGNES MONRO spovse to THOMAS /
VRQVHART of Kinbeachie who departed lyfe the 6 of Agovst 1661. / Blessed is
the / dead that dis / in the Lord they / rest from ther / labors and ther /* [works
do] *follow them."*) The armorial stone of his son John and John's wife, Isobel
Cuthbert of the Draikies family, is also there.
   Thomas Urquhart of Kinbeachie (died *c*1797) married Isobel Macleod and
had, among other children, John (1748-1831), Thomas (1752-1812 – he served
as Minister of Rosskeen 1784 to his death) and an illegitimate son (by a girl on
his estate) whom he named Alexander (died 1827; he became a ship's captain).
   John inherited Kinbeachie on the death of his father about 1797 but appears to
have been the black sheep of the family. A letter to Captain Thomas Urquhart
(who would become in due course Thomas Urquhart of Kinbeachie) from
brother Thomas, the Minister in Rosskeen, dated 21 April 1790 in Rosskeen
laments: *"Dear Nephew ... I am sorry to inform you that it wd. hurt your feelings
to hear of your Uncle John's conduct since he has broke thro' all restraint while
cash stood before him– he made himself a nausance to Society– a Disgrace to
humanity & was literally called an abomination in the Land – not only does he
Drink with the Rabble & Scum of the Creation but when he gets drunk is
perfectly insane Tears Bank Notes in pieces & throws them in the fire– In short
there is not one of his friends here that countenances him or ever wish to see him
or hear of him– oh! how galling how mortifying– all the Effects of vice of
dissipation and sin– and yet for 2 or 3 Weeks when in a private family is what he
ever was to appearance is such a deception– He has sold every Tree in
Kinbeachie tho' many of them are still standing– how Savage– & the Money*

amounting to upwards of a Hundred Pounds all gone & was it a thousand not a 6d. the day wd. he to the fore– ... He has spent within a few Pounds of £200 since his arrival here June last & none knows how except in the lowest Company of Gods Creation in Dissipation Madness & folly ... at Inverness the Publican was obliged to call for 4 Men to prevent his Committing Suicide."

This John Urquhart sold Kinbeachie to his half-nephew Thomas about 1818, and was looked after by a crofter's daughter in Brae before his death in 1831. His will is certainly the most unusual one to come out of a Resolis Proprietor: *"That I John Urquhart Esquire late of Kinbeachy at present residing at Brae, in the Parish of Resolis and County of Cromarty, for the love favor and affection which I have and bear to Jean Maclean daughter of John McLean Tenant in Brae, and on account of the great care and attention she has paid to me since I came to reside in her Fathers house, do hereby Leave and bequeath all the moveable property of whatever description, that may belong to me at the time of my death, to the said Jean McLean, whom I hereby nominate and appoint to be my sole Executor and universal Legatory."*

In fact, the remaining money amounted only to £92.12s.1d., although quite enough apparently for her new husband, Francis Mackenzie, a mason at Balblair, when removed from his tenancy by the Proprietor in 1837, to establish himself in a masonry business in Inverness.

Meanwhile, Thomas, having purchased Kinbeachie from his half-uncle John, married twice but had no children; he left Kinbeachie by entail to his nephew Thomas Urquhart (1823-1893). This Thomas married Mary MacNair Dryburgh Norrie in 1846 at Kiltearn and served as a Captain in the Crimean War; unable to make a financial success of Kinbeachie, they emigrated to and spent the remainder of their lives in Australia. When this Captain Thomas Urquhart of Kinbeachie died without an heir in 1893, Kinbeachie passed by entail to his cousin, Thomas Scrutton, whose son sold it in 1897.

The land at Kinbeachie is unusual within Resolis in that the Board of Agriculture took it over and created local smallholdings in 1923.

Kinbeachie Castle and the Kinbeachie Stone   NH63446218

Kinbeachie Castle, formerly a seat of the Urquharts, was demolished in 1959. It was a simple towerhouse within a courtyard. The south gable was the last part standing in a field at Kinbeachie (Cameron, the Resolis poet, described it as *"The old ruined gable that stands on the lea."*) The remains fortunately were photographed before demolition. It contained a fireplace over which was a panel dated 1546. At present the site is overgrown but the layout of the foundations can still be clearly seen.

The castle is associated with a carved sandstone slab, 1510 mm long by 830 mm wide, known as the Kinbeachie Stone. It was a fireplace overmantel in the hall in the old Castle of Cromarty, which was pulled down in 1772. It was subsequently within a house in Cromarty belonging to an Urquhart relative, but when that house was sold it was sent to Colonel Gordon as nearest of kin, who gave the stone to Mr Urquhart of Braelangwell. Captain Thomas Urquhart purchased the Kinbeachie Estate about 1818. Despite his link with the

Above, top: Kinbeachie Castle. From photograph courtesy of Mrs Essie Munro.
Above, bottom: Kinbeachie Stone.

Kinbeachie Urquharts being illegitimate, he took possession of the stone and installed it in Kinbeachie Castle. At some time, the relic was inserted into the side of a porch built onto one of a row of cottages occupied by workers on the farm. When the Board of Agriculture bought the Estate, it presented the stone to the Museum in Edinburgh.

This much-travelled stone is currently shown to great advantage in the National Museum of Scotland. Typical of a creation of the eccentric Sir Thomas Urquhart of Cromarty, it bears a profusion of symbols including the date 1651, harp-playing sirens, armoured knights on horseback and his initials, arms and motto, "*Meane Weil, Speak Weil and Doe Weil.*"

Kinbeachie Loch and Mill
Near to the remains of Kinbeachie Castle is the drained Kinbeachie Loch from which a lade supplied water to the mill near the Castle. The mill of Kinbeachie was of great antiquity – the following two references are 300 years apart:

"*Between the years 1565 and 1571 John bishop of Ross granted for life to Walter Vrquhart sheriff of Cromartie and Elisabeth M'Kenzie his wife, and to Henry Vrquhart their second son and his heirs male, with remainder to Walter's heirs whomsoever bearing the surname and arms of Vrquhart the lands of Kinbeachie extending to a half davach, the brewhouse of Kinbeachie with its croft, and the mill of Kinbeachie, then occupied by Walter and his tenants.*"

"*Inverness Journal 15 Jun 1827. Wanted, for the Mill of Kinbeachie, in the Parish of Resolis, a man who is competent to take charge of the Mills as Miller, to which is attached a considerable Thirlage.*"

The derelict Kinbeachie Mill attracted the poetic attention of Dick Cameron in the early 1900s; no trace of it now remains.

Kinbeachie charming
In 1737, Katherine McKenzie, spouse to John McKenzie tacksman in Kinbeachy, was excommunicated for her use of charms. She used them:

to prevent cattle straying in the high-lands "*first to repeat the creed & Lord's prayer & then to pray that they might be preserved & come safe home,*"

to make the cattle thrive and multiply "*Health follow my cow far or near as she goes, Mary's son that's able to make her ----, & to have a healthy calf*"

and also to make sick cattle recover and turn back envy "*The charm of God, the happy charm, the charm of Saint Malcolm who went to the Church, it went through the eyes of the people both weak & strong As ane evil eye harms the precious & humble of God, that they who have the evil eye their wishes may fall upon themselves, that the person who desires the greatest good may be drowned*" *in his blood, son of Envy the hollin bush fall upon their men fall upon their folds with cattell, upon their goods upon their sleep, upon their health, & upon their bed"* whilst blowing upon a small bowl of water, and then to throw the water towards the door of the person suspected of envy.

This third charm she learned from a transient Gairloch mother of twins. She had many years before spoken the charm and thrown the water against the door of James Clark her neighbour, tacksman in Kinbeachy, and immediately upon her doing of it, *"her own cow that was sick recovered, & her neighbour's cow suddenly after sickened & pined away for fourteen days, & then died."* She was put under the sentence of Excommunication for the sin of using charms, but she begged forgiveness and the sentence was lightened to satisfying discipline instead.

Kirkmichael – St Michael's Church Listed Scheduled **and churchyard** Listed
NH70596585
Arthur (1792) refers to the Gaelic *Keill-Mhichel* and Sage (1836) adds *"Its Gaelic name is* 'Kill a' Mhichail,' *or the Cell of St Michael; but this name is by the inhabitants usually given only to the church and burying-ground. The district which the ancient parish of Kirkmichael comprehended is called* 'Sgire' a' Mhichail,' *or the parish of St Michael."* Variants in various documents include Kyrimychel and Kylmichil. For history of the parish of Kirkmichael, see the section on Organised Religion, my booklet *"Kirkmichael – a Short History,"* and the Kirkmichael Trust website www.kirkmichael.info .

The Kirkmichael site is an historic treasure nestling in the Black Isle

Guided tour of Kirkmichael. Photograph by Andrew Dowsett.

countryside. It comprises the foundations of a pre-Reformation church, a medieval chancel, early 19th century nave/mausoleum, several mausolea of conservation value, and the graveyard itself, of which the earliest stones are of medieval date. The site is sadly partly derelict but a charity (The Kirkmichael Trust) has been established to transform it into an historical resource.

The earliest direct references to Kirkmichael are in Latin, within Vatican records. At this time in Scotland most church teinds had been appropriated by institutions. Both Kirkmichael and Cullicudden had been appropriated to the Cathedral of Ross by the 1400s. Legal disputes over the rights to the prebend (the shared revenues within a cathedral) were commonly referred to the Pope. This is where the name of Kirkmichael first appears in a written record, as the parish was the subject of long-standing disputes. The first mention of Kirkmichael thus comes in 1429, although the content of the reference implies its existence for at least some years previously.

Kirkmichael's first appearance on a map is on a Gordon manuscript map dated by the National Library of Scotland as *c*1637 (although this map may in fact be by Pont and hence may be a little earlier).

The Presbytery Minutes show that Kirkmichael was surprisingly often the venue for diets of the Presbytery (more often than most other churches of the Presbytery). They also show that the churches at Kirkmichael and Cullicudden were in use long after 1662, when the two parishes were amalgamated to form the modern parish of Resolis. Services alternated between the two old churches.

In 1741 the church at Kirkmichael was stated in the Minutes to be in good

Left: Medieval ornate cross, flanked by two swords. Photograph by Andrew Dowsett.
Above: 1725 McCulloch slab, rich with symbols of mortality.

condition (unlike the one at Cullicudden that was in this year stated in the Minutes to be unsafe for the congregation to meet therein). Indeed, in 1741 the option of enlarging Kirkmichael to serve the whole united parish instead of building a new church was advanced by some of the heritors. This was not agreed by the Presbytery, the objection being the hardship to the minister, whose manse and glebe were more than two miles distant to Kirkmichael; the Presbytery could not agree to it unless the Manse was removed to Kirkmichael and the Minister provided with as good a glebe as he already possessed.

The burial ground, of course, continued in use even after church activities transferred to Resolis in 1769.

In 1826 "*a complaint was lodged against John Holm the Kirk Officer by Evan Paterson son of Evan Paterson Crofter in St Martins lately deceased, stating that the Kirk Officer had overcharged him the said Evan Paterson for digging his fathers grave in the church yard of Kirk Michael. John Holm being called & interrogated, replied that the charge he had made was 5/- That is 3/- the usual rate for digging a grave & 2/- additional because the grave was opened in a new piece of ground in which there was no grave before & for the necessary & additional labour.*" The Kirk Session dismissed the complaint.

It was in this period that some of the main mausolea were initiated. The nave of the old church was rebuilt to some extent as a mausoleum for the Gun Munros of Poyntzfield about 1800.

The chancel already formed the mausoleum of the Urquharts of Braelangwell, as can be seen from the dates of the wall panels, one of which relates to a death in 1708.

The chancel also contains the grave of and memorial to William Gordon, whose body was originally buried in Rosskeen in 1778, but, as described by Hugh Miller, was later re-buried in this mausoleum by his sister Henrietta's husband, David Urquhart of Braelangwell – as a surprise gift for Henrietta! She had been pining at the thought of her brother languishing in the grave in Rosskeen.

The mausoleum also contains more recent memorials to the Shaw-Mackenzies of Newhall.

To the north of the church is the unusual Lady Ardoch tomb and to the south the extravagant Grant-Dunbar mausoleum, both described under Ardoch.

Kirkmichael has literary connections. An elegy by the author and poet Henry Mackenzie, famous in his day as the author of "*The Man of Feeling,*" is found on his friend William Gordon's memorial. Some of Hugh Miller's most emotive passages are associated with the attraction the site had for him. Another successful and more recent writer, Jane Duncan (Elizabeth Jane Cameron), is buried in the old part of the graveyard.

It was in the late 1820s that Hugh Miller worked in Kirkmichael; the stone he was employed on must be the Stewart tablestone to the north of the site.

Kirkmichael appears in several of his works, and he tells the following story of an earlier experience he himself had though he disguises himself.

"In the latter part of 1822 a young lad, a mason's apprentice, was employed with his master in working within the policies of Pointzfield – a gentleman's seat about a mile from the burying-ground. He wished much to visit the tombs and chapel, but could find no opportunity; for the day had so shortened that his employments engaged him from the first peep of light in the morning until half an hour after sunset. And perhaps the wish was the occasion of the dream. He had no sooner fallen asleep, after the fatigues of the day, than he found himself approaching the chapel in one of the finest of midsummer evenings. The whole western heavens were suffused with the blush of sunset – the hills, the woods, the fields, the sea, all the limbs and members of the great frame of nature, seemed enveloped in a mantle of beauty. He reached the burying-ground, and deemed it the loveliest spot he had ever seen. The tombs were finished after the most exquisite designs, chastely Grecian, or ornately Gothic; and myriads of flowering shrubs winded around the urns, and shaded the tablets in every disposition of beauty. The building seemed entire, but it was so encrusted with moss and lichens as to present an appearance of extreme antiquity; and on the western gable there was fixed a huge gnomon of bronze, fantastically carved like that of an antique dial, and green with the rust of ages. Suddenly a low breeze began to moan through the shrubs and bushes, the heavens became overcast, and the dreamer, turning towards the building, beheld with a sensation of fear the gnomon revolving slowly as on an axis, until the point rested significantly on the sward. He fled the place in deep horror, the night suddenly fell, and when floundering on in darkness and terror, through a morass that stretches beyond the southern wall of the chapel, he awoke, and lo! it was a dream. Only five weeks elapsed from this evening, until he followed to the burying-ground the corpse of a relative, and saw that the open grave occupied the identical spot on which the point of the gnomon had rested."

Kirkton Farm – Farm Buildings; Farmsteading   NH703661
Walker states that under episcopacy, the rector of Kirkmichael was also Archdeacon of Ross, possessing a fine manse immediately to the West of Fortrose Cathedral, and his glebe lands at Kirkton are said to have been the best in the whole parish.

An advertisement for letting Kirkton in 1818 describes it as: *"consisting of 189½ Acres of Arable Land, and 28 of Woodland and Moor Pasture, the greater part of which is capable of being improved at a trifling expence. This highly improved Farm, possesses many desirable advantages, having in the centre of the Lands, a neat House, and Garden, sufficient to accommodate a genteel Family; and Set of Offices in good repair, which for extent and convenience are surpassed by few in the Country. The Farm is bounded on the east by the Bay of*

Newhall, into which, the sea throws great quantities of drift sea-ware; and the beach abounds with small shell, shelly sand, and clay, which afford an inexhaustible stock of rich material for composts, and which, in skilful hands, would prove of incalculable benefit. The whole of these Lands have a south exposure; and the Wheat Crops produced from them, have always been considered of excellent quality. Coal and Lime are brought by sea to the beach, from which the produce of the Farm may be conveniently exported; and the Port of Cromarty, (at which all the Leith and London Traders, to and from Inverness, uniformly call for Freights, &c.) is only distant about six miles."

The tacksmen of Kirkton were important men in the area. They included Alexander Barkly (one of the Cromarty Barklys) who was tacksman from the late 1750s to 1788, when he moved into Barkly House from Kirkton after a quarrel with his in-laws, the Urquharts, who owned the farm at that time. There are several Barkly stones, and a Barkly enclosure, in Kirkmichael Burial ground.

From Newhall rentals (1755, 1762, 1772) Alexander Barkly's tenancy included the snuff mill built *"in the said Meikle Park"* at Kirktown. His rent included 2 lbs snuff yearly from the mill.

A foundling was abandoned by a heavily covered mystery woman one early morning in 1832. Originally from the parish, she had crossed the ferry from Fort George and walked all the way to Newhall, before turning off the main road to go up to Kirkton to lay the baby at the door of Donald McLean, tacksman of Kirkton, and one of the Church elders!

The boy was named Michael Martin after the two parish dedications – St Michael and St Martins. He got into trouble with another boy in 1845, whilst aged 13 and living in Gordonsmill. They had climbed through a window of the house of Robert Grigor, Esq. of Gordonsmill, to take – a portion of honey. He grew up to be a groom at Poyntzfield House.

The present buildings comprise a typical 19th century farmhouse and large planned farm (with later additions and alterations), but with the very unusual feature in the steading of a steam-engine chimney. Steam engines were rare enough away from coal-fields and this is one of very few in agricultural use. For the sequence of engines at Kirkton, see page 13.

Road up to Kirkton and the unusual sight of a farmstead with a boiler-house chimney.

The Laurels and West Laurels NH67606567, NH67196549
The first use of the name "*The Laurels*" I have found is in the 1920/1 Valuation
Roll. It has long been associated with the Robertson family.

Locherghil and the Oxgate of Lorgan
Two defunct names, the former occurring in the Church Register in the 1790s
and the latter mentioned in a 1694 document.

Millbuie
Gaelic: *Maol buidhe*, yellow rounded hill. Variants include Mulbuie, Millbuy.
There is no doubt from the profusion of archaeological remains found in the
heights of the Black Isle, including not only the cairns and settlements listed
under Brae, Woodhead, Culbo etc., but also artifacts such as the Group IX stone
axe found in the Millbuie, that the high ground was well populated from an early
date. In more recent history, the heights were used for common grazing, fuel and
roofing, and some quarries, until shared out amongst the estates in 1827. In more
recent times, there followed plantation forestry, through which walkers could
take long and secluded treks with occasional glimpses of the Firth through the
banks of trees. Much of the plantation forestry is now of harvest age, with multi-
use woodland replacing it, allowing more recreational scope. There is also scope
for interpretational resource here, if done correctly, including the crofthouses at
Agneshill, prehistoric sites, the abandoned quarries, regenerating moorland and
the history of the routes through the Black Isle.

The Break-up of the Mulbuie Commonty is described under Law and
Disorder but an interesting earlier incident is reported from the 1816 evidence.

The inhabitants of Fortrose routinely went to the Millbuie for turf and heather,
and had about 50 horses for that purpose. Witnesses recalled how on one
occasion (the evidence would suggest the early 1760s) "*having gone as far as
the property of Braelangwell or the burn of Auldaig, with these horses, for turf,
and there were others besides him, and Braelangwell seized them all, and
carried the horses to his court-yard; and that upon this being complained of to
the magistrates of Fortrose, they sent their town-clerk to protest against the
seizure and interruption, and the horses were sent back by Braelangwell; and, by
the authority of the magistrates, the inhabitants of Fortrose and Rosemarkie
went to that part of the moor where the interruption had taken place, and even
beyond it, and continued for a week cutting turf and pulling heather, and they
were never interrupted after that time.*" Other witnesses corroborated the clearly
rash seizure by Braelangwell of the horses and carts on the Millbuie.
Braelangwell was involved in dubious activity in the Millbuie again in 1810,
against which the minister sought redress from the Presbytery, when he was
settling tenants and developing extensive plantations of Fir (Scots Pine).

The Millbuie clearly presented a temptation to surrounding estates.

Milltoun
Variants Milton, Miltoun, Milntown.
Milltoun is shown on the Gordon *c*1637 map and the Blaeu 1654 map midway between Kirkmichael church and the confluence of the burns now called Allt Dubhach and Newhall Burn. Now obsolete. Some sources have suggested that the "*burn of Milltoun*" was Allt Dubhach but from the location of Milltoun it is more likely to have been Newhall Burn itself.

The Miln of Milntown of Rostobrichty, later Milntown of Newhall, according to 18th century sasines, was "*formerly called the Miln of Kintail.*"

Mount Eagle   NH64855901
I have not located the origins of the name of this, the highest point (256 m or 840 ft) in the Black Isle and Resolis. On the first edition 6 inch-mile OS map, the hill is called Cnoc nan Craiseag (Gaelic: *Craoiseag*, whortleberry); both are given on the modern 1:25,000 edition. However, there are references to an eagle stone (perhaps used as a boundary marker?) in this area in the 1816 Millbuy Commons plan. Could this be the origin? The Parishes of Avoch and Resolis meet at the summit of Mount Eagle, at an Ordnance Survey triangulation pillar within the forestry, close to a thicket of telecommunication masts.

Mount Eagle – Cnoc nan Craiseag – Cairn   NH648595
Scheduled. This cairn stands in a clearing in West Culbo Wood 1.4 km east of Upper Badrain farmhouse; it measures 9.8 m in diameter, 1.3 m in height and is surrounded by a ditch. In 1943, the RCAHMS noted a group of small cairns to the south and west of this cairn which is now inaccessible in dense woodland.

Mount High   NH698631
A hamlet of Forestry Commission dwellings, with a handy telephone box for those coming "*over Mount High*" from Rosemarkie. The land was compulsorily purchased from the Newhall Estate in 1933 by the Forestry Commission, and Forestry Commission holdings and Forester's House established later in the decade. On the first edition OS, Mount High originally was the name applied to a small building to the west of the road at Blackstand, just outside Resolis. A mystery worth exploring is why, on other mapping of this locality, the area to the east of the main road here is labelled "*Ardmeanach or Monk's Height.*"

The Neuk Name of recent origin.   NH65706505

Newfield, Newhall Bridge (Gean Cottage)   NH70366512
Originally Gean Cottage (*e.g.* 1901 Census), presumably due to the number of gean trees on the site, Newfield was the home of the Munro family of carpenters for several generations, the first being Angus Munro (see Literary Residents).

Newhall Estate   NH69836555 (Newhall House)
Thomas Urquhart, Minister of Ardersier, and a grandson of Thomas Urquhart of
Cromarty and Helen Abernethy, had two sons with Resolis connections: the
Reverend Thomas Urquhart of Braelangwell and Alexander Urquhart of Kinudie.
The latter purchased the Barony of Newhall and became Alexander Urquhart of
Newhall in 1670.

Neither Gordon's *c*1637 map nor Blaeu's 1654 map shows Newhall. The
former, however, includes "*Rostabrichty*," a name that commonly appears in
early documents, at the approximate location of Burnside of Newhall.
Rostabrichty with variant spellings continued in use within at least the Church
Register until the 1770s. The Milltown of Rosabrichtie became the Milltown of
Newhall; it is shown east of Rosabrichtie on Gordon's *c*1637 map. The Mill itself
seems to have been on the south side of the Newhall Burn, and fed by water
from the Ballicherry Burn. The Barony of Newhall at this time included the
Ward of Gelnie (the Newhall Burn was the Water of Gelnie), Wester Balblair, the
Mill of Milntown and the Lands of Roseabrighty.

In 1678, Alexander Urquhart of Newhall with his son John and the Laird of
Cromarty were Commissioners to the Scottish Parliament. The family was in that
year at its most prosperous, and thereafter it gradually declined. The estate then
consisted of about 9,000 acres of land. Both Alexander and his son John were
buried at Kirkmichael, but the location of their graves is not known. John's son,
Lt.-Colonel Alexander Urquhart of Newhall, MP for Cromarty, was ruined in the
South-Sea Bubble in 1720, and was also involved in the Darien Scheme. He died
in 1727 and the estate was sequestrated. His son Captain David Urquhart,
nominally last of Newhall, but never, strictly speaking, of Newhall at all, died in
1754. Newhall passed to the Gordons, the main creditors.

The first "*Gordon of Newhall*" was Charles Hamilton Gordon, a prominent
lawyer, who died in 1761. His son William Gordon also inherited Wester St
Martins, Easter and Wester Balblair, and Meikle and Little Braes, and is buried
in Kirkmichael (having been initially buried in Rosskeen! – see Kirkmichael)
with an epitaph by Henry Mackenzie, author of "*The Man of Feeling.*"

On William's early death at 22, his sister Henrietta, then Lockhart, inherited in
1778 all the above; her second husband was David Urquhart of Braelangwell
(1748-1811), continuing an Urquhart connection with Newhall. Henrietta was
noted for improving the estate (Gordonsmills, Henrietta Park) and rebuilding
both Newhall and Braelangwell Houses in the Adam style. She died in 1799, at
an early age, and a graceful eulogy can be found on her memorial in Kirkmichael.

Walker now picks up the story: "*One of the Gordons had married a relative of
Mackenzie of Coul, and their eldest son, Colin Mackenzie Dhu, merchant in
London, left £40,000 for the purchase of Newhall and other entailed lands by
will dated 1798. His nephews, Donald and Colin, both died without issue, and by
entail Newhall had to go to the nearest male heir on the death of Colin in 1842.*

The fifth sister of Colin Mackenzie Dhu had married John Stewart, Episcopal minister in Inverness, and their daughter, Charlotte Stewart, became the wife of Alexander Shaw of Tordarroch, tenth Chief of Ay, and later Lieutenant-Governor of the Isle of Man. Newhall was inherited by Charlotte's grandson, John Andrew Shaw, formerly of the Honourable East India Company, and on his succession he assumed the name of Shaw-Mackenzie. He was himself succeeded in 1886 by his nephew, Charles Forbes Hodson Shaw-Mackenzie, a Judge in Bombay Presidency 1862-1885, whose grandson was in 1957 officially recognised as sixteenth Chief of Ay, with surname Shaw of Tordarroch." The ancient barony of Newhall passed by entail first to his elder daughter, and then to his eldest grand-daughter, Rebecca, who retains the name of Shaw-Mackenzie. Details can be found in *"A History of Clan Shaw"* by Major C.J. Shaw of Tordarroch.

Ash describes how the later Mackenzies established an approach to resettling tenants that was beneficent and shaped the look of the parish. An estate map of 1849 at Newhall shows clusters of small crofts of between 3 and 11 acres lining the county road between the Bog of Cullicudden and Resolis, thus creating the linear settlement pattern of small croft houses that still largely exists. These Newhall crofts were rent-free for 25 years and 2/6 an acre thereafter. As an earlier (1813) estate map at Newhall shows the beginning of enclosure and improvement on the estate, including creation of large fields over rigs in places such as Castlecraig and Cullicudden, Ash suggests the change in estate planning to create smallholdings was a direct response to clearances elsewhere.

The estate of Newhall was largely put up for sale in 1918, although Newhall House, with extensive curtilage, yet remains with the family.

Newhall House Listed   NH69836555
Newhall House, an impressive Georgian mansion in the style of Adam, was built for Captain Donald MacKenzie in 1807. The architect was James Smith of Inverness. The front steps were enlarged and marble stones for chimney purchased in 1819. It incorporates to the rear an earlier house begun in 1725 for Alexander Urquhart of Newhall, but which passed to the Gordon family shortly after completion. Urquhart's house had, in turn, replaced an earlier building, ruinous by 1730. A 1788 estate plan shows vignettes of both the new house (of that time) and Old House of Newhall, the latter placed beside a vignette of the old Mill of Newhall and fairly close to the entrance way and public road.

The gateway to Newhall House lies to the north side of Newhall Bridge. Like the House, the gate piers and the gates are listed. Walker refers to a legend of an underground cell or dungeon near the gateway, perhaps simply repeating the suggestion on page 29 of *"The old sherriffdom of Cromarty"* by W.M. Mackenzie (1922) that *"A Pit or Dungeon under the Bridge of Newhall"* was used as a prison in the 17th-18th centuries. However, there is no other documentary support for the existence of such a feature, the Bridge of Newhall is

more recent than the 18ᵗʰ century and in inquiries carried out in 1966 Major
Shaw had never heard of a dungeon in that area. A pit or dungeon in this boggy,
often-flooded location would have been a rather damp choice!

The present house is a classical mansion with Doric portico and pedimented
frontage with a three-light window centre first-floor. It comprises two storeys
and a basement, built in a rectangle of five bays by five, and has a piended
platform roof. An unusual faceted sundial stands to its front.

Mains of Newhall Listed   NH69536560

To the west of Newhall is Newhall Mains, a handsome courtyard of farm
buildings, with central archway under a pyramid-roofed pigeon loft or doocot
topped by a curiously-shaped weathervane. At present, the building is gutted, but
there is clearly much scope for imaginative conversion.

Newhall Burn and Newhall Bridge   NH70236520 (Newhall Bridge)

The Newhall Burn has its source at Kinbeachie and once drove mills at
Kinbeachie, St Martins, Newmills and Gordon's Mill, before entering Udale Bay.

Many old documents refer to the Water of Gelnie or Gelny, which is the name
that the Newhall Burn had in this location; the Ward of Gelnie therefore must
have been land close to the Burn.

There has long been a smiddy at the Bridge – the Church Registers mention a
Gilbert Urquhart, blacksmith at the Bridge of Newhall, from 1851 onwards.

Although rarely seen, there is a second arch of Newhall Bridge, which was re-
excavated during works following the 2006 flood. The burn is prone to flood.
Donald Sage one evening in 1825 arrived at the bridge to find that the burn had

Newhall House.

swollen alarmingly. "*It had cut out a new channel on the north side of the bridge, so as to preclude all possibility of crossing.*" After another abortive attempt to cross at a ford north east of Braelangwell, he gave up and sought shelter overnight at Poyntzfield House.

Willis tells a story of the Bodach's Bridge – the bridge over the Newhall Burn – dating back to the end of the 18th century. The bridge was regarded as an eerie

Doocot, Newhall Mains.

Newhall Bridge with Smiddy behind; the Newhall Burn in quiet mood.

The Newhall Burn causing the road to collapse and gouging out a new channel in 2006 just as Sage witnessed in 1825.

place to cross in the dark hours, and one night a local man was coming up the rise of the bridge and met at the top a strange apparition, appearing to be a lady dressed in finery, a brown silk dress and high-heeled shoes. The apparition halted him and told him the specific time of when he would die. The man's friends, when he informed them of this next day, told him to dismiss the incident as a brainstorm but the dread took hold of him to such an extent that he sickened and died, passing away on the very day the apparition had predicted!

Newhall Primary School – see Education.   NH69126535

Newmills – Mill and Mobile Threshing Machines   NH67786471
Newmills is the name of the area surrounding the former mill complex at this location. Only the empty buildings of the complex survive. The mill was fed by a long lade that crossed the Church Brae to the north of the Free Church.
   Walker suggests that Henrietta Gordon *"must have been responsible for*

Top: My uncle, William Munro, and his Traction Engine at Newmills.
Bottom: Feeding the mill at Gordonsmill, 1940s, with Willie's Engine at full power.
Photographs courtesy of Mrs Sheila Macdonald, Avoch.

moving the old estate mill to its present position at Newmills" but I note there are records of Newmills or Newmiln of Resolis from at least the early 1740s, before Henrietta was born. Alston notes that the present complex was built in the 1830s to replace earlier mills. My father mentioned it was ideally designed as it was easy to drop grain down into from above.

The mills were run by the Munro family (previously millers at Kinbeachie) for much of the 20th century, and they also ran several mobile steam and modern threshing machines. When "*the mill*" arrived at a farmyard, it was a great event, with the farm workers cutting sheaves and feeding them into the mill from the stacks in the farmyard, and every child in the area waiting with a stick to pounce on the inevitable swarm of rats that would appear, often en masse, as the stack reached the base, with inevitable chaos as dogs would join the fray.

Park Cottage   NH667650
This small cottage, to the west of the Church Brae close to Resolis Crossroads, was occupied by Davy Whyte in the 1950s-1960s, but is now demolished.

Poyntzfield Estate   NH71076425 (Poyntzfield House)
As mentioned under Ardoch, George Munro had on 29 May 1760 married the heiress widow Mary Hinde ms Poyntz and became in due course Sir George Gun Munro of Poyntzfield. He purchased Ardoch in 1761 and renamed it Poyntzfield.

Previous sources have incorrectly identified Munro's bride as a) Charlotte Hyde ms Poyntz, b) Jemima Poyntz, daughter of a Dutch father and an English Mother, c) Anna Maria Poyntz and d) Georgiana Poyntz, a forebear of Princess Diana. Much investigation of original material followed as I tried to identify the lady, and then as luck would have it I found two separate reliable sources at the same time. Litigation records in the Public Record Office in Kew and her re-married mother's will both independently confirmed she was Mary Poyntz, daughter of Deane Poyntz, a merchant in Jamaica, and Florence Fulton. Her first husband, George Hinde, owned much land in Kent and Jamaica. Full details can be found in the paper listed in the References.

There was indeed a Princess Diana connection. Mary's uncle was the Right Honourable Stephen Poyntz, a diplomat, and it was his youngest daughter Georgina Margaret who married in 1755 John Spencer. He became in 1761 Baron and Viscount Spencer of Althorp, and later Earl Spencer and Viscount Althorp. The link was thus made between the Poyntz and Spencer families. HRH William's 6-great grandfather and grandmother were Stephen and his wife, Anna Maria, Lady Mary Munro's uncle and aunt.

Poyntzfield was entailed, and passed, on the death of the childless Sir George Gun Munro, to his nephew George Gun Munro (II). George (II) had been declared bankrupt in London and Sir George before his death had gone to some lengths designing a legal structure for inheritance to ensure that his debtors would not be able to seize the estate. The nephew seemed to spend much of his life in legal entanglements.

George (II) had an illegitimate son, also named George Gun. Fortrose Academy was built in 1791, and in a letter of August 1791 George (II) is thinking of sending young George to the new school in Fortrose of which he was hearing good things. The son rose to become Treasurer of the Island of Grenada (on which there was a plantation estate named Poyntzfield) and the Inverness Journal of 28 June 1811, recording donations to the Academy of Fortrose, mentions that *"George Gunn Munro, treasurer of the Island of Grenada, son of Mr Munro of Poyntzfield, and an old pupil, had sent £210."*

It was George (II) who rebuilt the nave of Kirkmichael as a mausoleum. His uncle, Sutherland of Rearquhar, writes: *"George Gun Munro of Poyntzfield Died upon Wednisday 2nd July 1806 & was buryd in a Burying Ground he himself built when his uncle Sir George Munro his Predecessor, & Lady Munro Died: His Widow by an agreemt. with his Br. Col. Ines Munro (who Succeeded him as he died without Issue) continued in Poyntzfield to Whit.sy 1807. When Col: Inness enterd upon the Possession &c. She retired to a house of her own in Foress."*

Without a legitimate heir, the estate next passed to George (II)'s brother, Colonel Innes Gun Munro. He married Anne Gordon, and his eldest surviving son, Sir George Gun Munro (III), an army Major, succeeded him.

Sir George was *"a man of broad views and great public spirit. He, like his grandfather, executed many improvements on his estate, and did much to advance the educational interests of the parish of Resolis. He, at his own expense, built and kept in repair a school and schoolmaster's house in*

Poyntzfield House
from the front.

Poyntzfield House
from the rear.

Jemimaville, so called after his wife, long before the days of School Boards, and had the honour of Knighthood conferred upon him in 1842 in acknowledgment of his liberality and public spirit. He married, in 1822, Jemima Charlotte, daughter of Colonel Dundas Graham, Cromarty House..."

Imaginatively, he named his heir and successor George Gun. George (IV) was born in 1828, but died, unmarried, in 1860, and was succeeded by his brother Captain Innes Colin Munro. In turn, Captain Munro's son, Captain George Mackenzie Gun Munro became his heir and successor.

There is an interesting 1771 memorial to the Commissioners of Supply from Poyntzfield, in which he seeks to be appointed as principal surveyor and overseer for making and repairing "*all the high Roads within the County of Cromarty that part of it lying in the black Isle* [the earliest reference I have found to the name Black Isle in Resolis sources] *with a Suitable allowance.*" He seeks the support of the County to assist "*in bringing out their Tennants & all others residing within the County to work on the Roads, the Six days (ordered by Act of Parliam^t.) all at once, in place of going on the Roads in Octr when the harvest Work is over, as no work can be forwarded in that late Season of the Year in this Northern Climate.*"

Poyntzfield House Listed   NH71076425

The estate of Ardoch was owned by Alexander Gordon, whose wife was Ann Munro, a daughter of the laird of Foulis. It has been suggested that this may account for some similarities between this house – built before 1757 by their son Adam Gordon – and the Munro castle at Foulis.

The mansion was built in 1720 as a two-storey house with wings, raised to three storeys in 1757 with a new room above the stair tower. This is the date on the corbel heads, below the small pediment on the west front. Further work was done in 1775 and 1790 adding drawing and dining rooms. The mansion forms three sides of a square courtyard, with at the back the attractive feature of an octagonal look-out tower (known as Jemima's Tower) with an ogee-domed slate roof. The figure standing atop the tower is a recent addition.

There are two old sundials in the garden, one either side of the house. From the commercial herb nursery in the walled garden, open from spring to autumn, the back of the house can be seen. At the end of the north drive are corniced and ball-finialled gatepiers, contemporary with the house, which are also listed.

Poyntzfield Mills – Mill complex   NH70676374

This mill complex, along the north drive to Poyntzfield House, is considered as unusual and important. The Scottish Vernacular Buildings Working Group 1989 Conference Proceedings contain a description and drawings. In the 1870s, the OS notes both a corn (*i.e.* meal) mill and a flour mill. In 1906, on the 2nd edition OS map, there is mention only of a corn mill. By 1930, the mills were disused.

The water was brought down from the mill pond by means of an aqueduct, powering first the wheel on the flour mill and then, via a second aqueduct, the wheel on the meal mill below. The Black Isle was noted for wheat growing, thus explaining the presence of a flour mill, otherwise rare this far north.

The flour mill, now converted to a house, has a cross on one of its crow-stepped gables (in the 1870s, the OS records a cross on both gables), for some as yet unknown but presumably religious intention.

Poyntzfield – Whisky Distillery

Mr Duncan Montgomery advertised in 1816 that he was about to start selling whisky from a Distillery established at Poyntzfield, but warned that he could only make a success of it if Magistrates and Landlords would make a concerted effort in putting a stop to Illicit Distillation. A further advertisement in 1823 selling off all the distillation equipment at Poyntzfield speaks for itself. However, Montgomery did claim in his bankruptcy proceedings that stocking and cropping the farm at the mains of Poyntzfield as well as establishing the Distillery had contributed to his becoming *"a considerable loser particularly by the Farm which he found in the most wretched order, and it defied him yet to put it in proper condition."*

Poulnasuiack

A name I have come across but once – on the 1826 Militia List, with numerous residents listed with trades (*e.g.* Peter Fraser maltster) indicating that the location was a distillery; the same people reoccur under Braelangwell in the 1828 and 1831 Militia Lists; and Peter Fraser is maltsman at Brealangwell on the christening of two of his children in November 1827 and May 1829. This evidence strongly suggests that the location of the distillery at Braelangwell was formerly known as Poulnasuiack.

Poyntzfield Flour Mill
with cross on
crowstepped gable,
and the Meal Mill below.
The waterwheels were on
the far side of the buildings.

Railway – The Cromarty & Dingwall Light Railway
Authorised by Act of Parliament in August 1902, but with the first sod cut on 13
February 1914, the Cromarty & Dingwall Light Railway was doomed to fail. Six
miles of track were laid, but the First World War intervened, the track was
uplifted during the war, and the construction was eventually abandoned. The
land had been set aside for the railway (carefully avoiding the estate houses) and
even now the line can be traced via Jemimaville (hidden bridge beside garage),
Braelangwell (the "*Bridge to Nowhere*") and the bridge and cutting at
Cullicudden (see Sunnylea), with various other bridges, embankments and
fencing. See page vii for photographs and References for a Booklet.

The Red Gate or The Red Gates   NH693662 (north end)
This is the name given to the road that runs from Sheep Park down to Newhall
steading. At the Newhall end, two red gates did indeed once stand, and a recess
for a gate post can still be seen in a wall just before a cartshed. When I was
young, walking along to Auchmartin with my brothers and sister, passing the
Red Gate was a dreaded experience because of all the stories we'd been told
about the ghostly Green Lady said to frequent the track.

Resolis
Gaelic: *Ruigh-sholuis*, slope of light, or bright slope.
Resolis existed as a settlement long before the parishes of Kirkmichael and
Cullicudden were united with a new church to be built at a centrical location. It
is mentioned in Pont's description of the area in the 1580s/90s and a sasine of
1628, and was important enough to be identified on Gordon's *c*1637 map and
Blaeu's 1654 map. The new church, manse and glebe at Resolis inevitably led to
the name of Resolis becoming associated with the parish.
     Within the parish, Resolis can be applied to the small district bounded by
Cullicudden and Ferryton on the west and east respectively, and extending on
both sides of the B9163 rather unevenly to include **Resolis Mains**, **Resolis
Cottage** and **Bog of Resolis**.
     A strange legal case involved a tenant in this area. In 1831, John Hossack, late
Tenant in Resolis petitioned the Kirk Session for "*a certificate of Poverty &
Character to enable him to be put upon the Poors Roll in order to institute an
action before the supreme court*" against the Newhall Estate.
     However, the Session refused to give a good character reference, a declaration
being made by John Murray, the Newhall Ground Officer, that John had
assaulted his brother twice to the danger of his life. In support of this, Donald
Holm, a mason and cottar in Resolis, declared that one day when he was building
a Pig Sty at the farm of Resolis: "*John Hossack the Petitioner & his brother
Joseph Hossack, with their Cow Herd were along with him assisting him, that
John Hossack ordered the boy to put on some straw from the stable loft, that his*

brother Joseph told the Boy before he fetched the straw to bring some clay. That upon this John Hossack flew into a passion at his brother Joseph & took up a stone to throw at him. That Joseph Hossack bent his head to avoid the stone thrown at him, upon which John Hossack took up a stone hammer to strike his brother, who immediately ran in to the stable to avoid him. That John Hossack pursued his brother Joseph into the stable & from the stable into the House with the Hammer in his hand & that Joseph Hossack only escaped being struck by the Petitioner John Hossack at last by getting into the House & bolting the door against him."

Donald Junor, Tacksman at Resolis, declared that during harvest he was called *"to come & separate the two brothers John & Joseph Hossack who, he was told were fighting with each other on the Potato field."*

This case was more serious than at first sight appears, as 1831 was a time when the Newhall Estate's purge of tenants reached new heights, and undoubtedly the evidence here was to prevent Hossack from being able to take retributive legal action.

Resolis Church Listed   NH67866548
The architect and date are given as James Boag and 1767, although it was repaired many times and remodelled 1830 to replace its small and dark windows with the present tall windows. It is a plain rectangular church with unusual rear elevation, built against a slope to which it is linked by paired porches with cat-

Resolis Church, access to   Removing pews to a
the gallery, with cat-slide roof.   safe home in the parish.

slide (sloping) roofs giving first-floor access to the gallery. From the lairds' pews at the front of the gallery, the lairds were unable to be viewed by their tenants in the pews below.

The bell by George Watt of Edinburgh is initialled DU HG 1787 (David Urquhart/Henrietta Gordon of Braelangwell). On its closure in 2006, a silent auction was held to empty the church of its moveable contents, so its clock and some of its pews, desks and other furniture remain in the parish.

The fine pulpit (for photograph, see page 38) with ogee sounding board, commemorating the Reverend Hector McPhail, minister of Resolis parish (1748-74), passed to an antiques shop. Walker states that originally a *"double-decker"* pulpit, it had the precentor's box removed in 1930, when a harmonium was brought in from the former United Free Church; and the original long Communion Table down the centre aisle was replaced in 1925 with a small modern Table, and gives more details on the contents of the church.

The old pews in the gallery were marked with letters and numbers to indicate the farms on the various estates to which they were allotted; no seat rents were charged, but a sum of 14s. to 16s. per seat was originally paid to the heritors and repaid by the incoming to the outgoing tenant.

Communion services were held on the uncultivated area to the north west of the junction of Fanny's Brae and the church road. At time of writing, the former church (sold 2005) is being converted to a house.

Resolis Parish Manse   NH67906542
The first manse at Resolis was very small and situated on marshy ground at the bottom of the brae, but in 1831 the present manse was built on a much more commodious scale. Designed and built, in partnership with Donald Munro of Tain, by John Rose of Invergordon, 1830-2. Sold 1985; now a private residence.

Glebe of Resolis – building, stone cup   cNH679655
Sage (1836) mentions that when the circular base of an ancient Pictish house, on the glebe of Resolis, was trenched over about 1834, about 1½ feet (46 cm) below the surface a handled stone cup was found, possessed by himself. However, the location of neither site nor cup is now known.

Resolis Free Church Listed   NH67266455
The second Free Church in Resolis, by William Munro and Andrew Maitland, 1865. Harled, with round-arched windows and lattice glazing. The west gable contains a *"ball-finialled birdcage bellcote."* The great beams in the roof came to the pier at Alness Ferry and were transported by horse and cart from there. Renovated in recent years, with the pews replaced by modern seating, freshly painted and panelled, and with effective heating installed, it is infinitely more comfortable and welcoming than in its original austere form.

Resolis Free Church Manse   NH67296449
An attractive, two-storey manse with small front gable, on the north bank of the
Newhall Burn, by Andrew Maitland & Sons, 1880; now a private residence.

Resolis Memorial Hall   NH68256503
Resolis is rightly proud of its distinguished Memorial Hall, completed in 1959.
The Hall was entirely funded by community effort, on land given over from the
Newhall Estate by Major Shaw of Tordarroch; even the previous booklet on the
history of the parish by the Church of Scotland minister of the time, George
Walker, was "*in aid of the War Memorial Hall.*" The imposing front and side
doors were from the famous Rosehaugh House.

The previous hall had been a wooden hut in the wood nearby on the south side
of the road, and was in ramshackle condition by the end, although it too had been
the social centre of the parish since the first world war.

The Memorial Hall, and its associated extensive playing area, became one of
the centres of parish life, with popular concerts, dramas, school gatherings,
badminton and other sports inside, and sports days outside, talks, dances
(including the famous "*Dance 'til Dawn*") and public events of all types, with the
Hall Committee even organising the well-attended Resolis Sheepdog Trials. In
later years, grants permitted an extension which gave improved catering
arrangements, and at time of writing there has been a successful bid for funding
an all-weather playing surface.

As the hall was unlicensed, drinkers were known to adjourn temporarily to the
Balblair Ferry Inn for refreshment, and local lads would be on the steps outside
as bouncers to discourage drink being carried inside. Like many other rural halls,

Resolis Memorial Hall, opened 1959.

eventually the level of disturbance, often associated with groups from outside the area, ended the public dances, although these continue by invitation only.

Many of the activities of local groups such as the very successful CRU Club (the Young Farmers Club for Cromarty, Resolis and Urquhart), Women's Guild, WI, Resolis Under-5s and sports groups centred on the Parish Hall.

In recent years the Hall has established itself as a presence on the arts circuit, with international names in the field of music appearing to audiences drawn in from a wide area.

Resolis – Ring-Ditch and Cropmarks   NH671652

In 1995, oblique aerial photography revealed cropmarks of part of a ring-ditch 200 m south west of Resolis farmsteading. The visible northwest side of the ring-ditch suggests it has an internal diameter of about 18 m to 20 m. Indeterminate cropmarks are scattered across the surrounding field.

Rose Cottage

There appear to have been at least two Rose Cottages in Resolis, both appearing in the 1901 Census, one at Newhall (occupied by blacksmith John Munro) and one in Jemimaville (occupied by midwife Catherine Robertson); the Jemimaville housename still exists.

Rostabrichty or Rosabrighty

Rostabrichty was situated, according to Blaeu's map, a little to the north west of Braelangwell, close to the modern location of Burnside; later Rosabrighty, 1740. The land around Rosabrighty became the Barony of Newhall.

Rowan Cottage   NH65786461

Another botanical name, first appearing on the 1901 Census. At that time, it was occupied by Andrew McKenzie, a house carpenter, originally from Agneshill, known as "*Andrew Cheese.*" His nickname came from his catchphrase – when he was sawing wood, he would say he was going through it "*like going through cheese.*" His whole large family became known as Cheese: there was Tom Cheese, Willie Cheese, Alasdair, Jack and Jessie Cheese.

A local shop was opened here by the Fraser family in the 1920s, closing sometime after 1945, selling groceries and butcher meat. When it opened, Mr Fraser (known as "*Ouncie*" from being very exact at the weighing machine) took a pony and cart around as a van.

Shawfield Cottage   NH70286551

Part of the Newhall Estate and presumably named after the Shaw family. Shawfield Cottage appears on the 1901 Census.

Sheeppark   NH69116667
The first reference I have noted is in 1808, when it is given as "*Sheep park (part of Ferrytown)*" and possessed by Thomas & George McKeddie with a rental of 30 Bolls meal and £5.

Long associated with the Macdonalds, farmers and ferrymen. James S ("*Jeemie*") Macdonald Sheeppark had served in Gallipoli during the First World War and was Commander of the Homeguard in Resolis during the Second World War, but his Homeguard men didn't make his life easy. Shooting practice was at the hillside at Sheeppark – the story goes that the famous roadmen, Jock and Barney "*Tunach*" couldn't get out of the house all day Saturday because of the bullets flying past the house. The Homeguard then built a sand barrier to contain the firing, but it was not very well made, for, to save effort, some bags were filled with bracken instead of sand! Another story is of a famous parade when several of the Homeguard appeared with virtually only the uppers left on their boots. The farmworkers in the troop couldn't obtain working boots during the war and had been using them (and their uniforms too) at farmwork.

St Martins – Estate, Mill and Smiddy
St Martins appears in an entry in 1557 in the Register of the Great Seal, but clearly the name must have existed long before this time. It should be noted that Easter and Wester St Martins were at times under different ownership, and that much of the area now considered St Martins was Drumcudden. Early documents including St Martins always refer to it as with an ale-house.

From the Bishop of Ross, St Martins passed to the Urquharts. Families thereafter associated with St Martins include the Gordons, the Dallas family (who held St Martins for the late part of the 17th century until selling it in 1696), and Fraser of Brae. It came into the Braelangwell estate, in the papers of which its history can be traced, including the origins of the "*Lyon-Mackenzies of St Martins and Braelangwell.*"

All that remains of St Martins Mill are the remnants of the walls beside the bridge at NH64946338. Water was led northward off Kinbeachie Burn to a mill pond and then on to the mill, the layout clearly seen on first edition OS. It has been suggested that the undergrowth to the west of the bridge may harbour the remains of a much older mill.

A photograph of the mill *c*1906 can be seen in Uncle's "*Easter Ross and the Black Isle*" – St Martins Smiddy also appears in the background. This Smiddy stood below where the house appropriately called Edgemill now stands, close to the mill. The Smiddy ceased when the then occupiers (Ross) moved to Balloan Farm near Culbokie in 1847. Elec "*the Botch*" Ross also charged batteries and sold a wide variety of articles from the Smiddy, including workclothes and even wedding dresses. There was a fuss once when the bride turned her dress over to find a big black handprint on the back!

St Martins – Burial Ground   NH63606262
The modern St Martins Burial Ground lies below the old tree-lined track that originally ran from Kinbeachie through to Cullicudden Church. It is a peaceful, sheltered location.

St Martins (Drumdyre) – Church; Burial-ground; Well
The site associated with St Martin's Church and St Martin's Well is now included in the land of the farm of Drumdyre. In 1966, the footings of a building measuring 14 m from east to west by 7 m transversely with an annexe about 4.6 m square on the north east were measured, and these remains can still be seen on the ground (NH64566267). At the same time, it was recorded that the "*trouty well,*" a natural spring, measured 0.6 m square, by 0.9 m deep, had a cover stone, and lay immediately to the west – this too still remains (NH64546262). For photography, see section on Organised Religion.

There is no trace of a burial ground in the vicinity of the church. Although threatened with removal in the 1960s for agricultural purposes, the church footings were still evident at time of writing. Archaeological investigation would undoubtedly reveal valuable information.

Walker states that the Church was dedicated to Martin of Tours and that popular tradition suggested it was once served by monks from Beauly Priory. He, and other writers, have hypothesised that this Church was the original church of the parish of Cullicudden, and the later ruin at Cullicudden, with its datestone of 1609, replaced it. However, the evidence suggests that the site at Cullicudden was in use long before 1609 and it is now considered possible that it represents the site of the original church, leaving the origins of St Martins obscure.

Other guides have referred to the church of St Martins lying waste in 1641 but I note that the Register of the Great Seal of Scotland in 1591/2 names several annual fairs in the Black Isle, including one on 10 November, the Martinmas fair, which was held of old at the church of St Martins in Ardmannoch now lying waste. This pushes the dereliction of St Martins 50 years further back.

The Inverness Burgh Court Books describe how in November 1566 three men were found guilty of "*forestalling,*" especially at St Martin's Fair in Ardmannoch. They pleaded in defence that this Fair was a free market at which it was lawful to all manner of men to buy and sell, but the Court found that such a right had been given by the Kings of Scotland to the Burgh of Inverness only, "*quha hes the libertie of the haill schire to suffer sic wayeris to cum to the said kirk* [*i.e.* St Martins]." The Fair at St Martins kirk was thus operational in 1566.

An intriguing description of the area in Macfarlane's Geographical Collections, from what were probably Timothy Pont's papers (hence 1580s/1590s), states: "*half a myl therfra Findounbeg. ½ myl thence Findown moir. ½ moir thence Langreid. 2 myl thence Kilmartyn with a kirk. half myl thence Drumwhiddin. ½ myl therfra Cullecuddin with a kirk. ½ myl thence Craighous with a tour of 4 hous height.*" This at least confirms the co-existence of the two churches, although the relationship between the two has yet to be discovered.

St Martins – charming
The Presbytery records for 1734 contain an example of charming by a St Martins resident: "*there was given in a Referance from the Session of Cullicuden anent Donald Simson Shoemaker in St Martins Bearing Date the seventh of March Current Shewing that the Said Donald Simson being Cited to their Meeting of the Said Day for going in to the Cornyeard of Donald Davidson & John Murray in Drumcudden & fetching away thence some Earth with him in a Clandestine way or manner which lookt like Charmeing or Sorcery whereupon he was Called & Compearing was Interrogate if he had so Done: He Confessed he did and lodged the Said Earth in his own Cornyeard to the End the Substance of the Said Donald Davidson & John Murray their Cornyeard might be transferred to him.*" Simson stated that he had learned the practice from "*a transient beggar who had lodged at his house the night before.*" The Presbytery Moderator "*having Seriously Dealt with him Anent & warned of the Complex Nature & heinousness of his Sin as Containing the Sins of Envy Avarice Discontent & witchcraft he was remitted to the said Session to Satisfy Discipline in usual form.*"

Springfield   NH670639 (general area)
Name in use from at least 1798 (Church Register) (see also Cnoc Topach). "*Harry Spring*" was a lady (Harriet Fraser, Springfield) who was well-off and bought a line of houses in Alness now known as Springfield Terrace.

Sunnylea   NH66126437
Named when purchased from the Newhall Estate in 1920. One of the few remaining sections of the Cromarty to Dingwall Railway can be seen here, a cutting curving south east from the railway bridge at the access to Sunnylea.

The railway line crossing the Cullicudden Straight at the entranceway to Sunnylea.
From the 1918 Newhall Estate Sale Plan.

Teannafed A location noted in the Church Register in 1757 but now defunct.

Tighninnich
Gaelic: *Tigh 'n aonaich*, town of the market. Walker states: *"During the last century a market used to be held at Tighninnich, between Jemimaville and Balblair."* As the name of Tighninnich (and variants) is much earlier, appearing on Gordon *c*1637 and Blaeu 1654 and a sasine of 1644, there must have been a market here in medieval times.

Toberchurn   NH620625 (general area); NH61956291 (the spring itself)
Gaelic: *Tobar a' Chuirn*, Well of the cairn.
There is a disposition (dated 13 September 1666) by Hugh Monro of Findon in favour of Sir John Urquhart of Cromartie of the Wester part and portion of the Lands of Toberchurne with the Grazings &c. thereof in the Parish of Cullicudden which pertained formerly to the deceased Alexander Urquhart of Craighouse and were wadset and disponed by him to Neill Munro of Findon the Granters father.

OS mapping (1870s) shows the Foulis Ferry landing place within Resolis, on the shore at Toberchurn, with the ferry track up the brae to Wester Toberchurn, and the Signal Board at Toberchurn, used to call the attention of the boatman at Foulis. However, a 1769 Findon estate plan shows the Ferry more to the west and the Urquhart OSA (1742) refers to the ferry, so it must have shifted east.

The Fraser family have farmed Toberchurn for a long time. In probably the first motoring offence in Resolis, Samuel Clarkson, Shooting Tenant, Cromarty Estate, was fined 10s in 1906 for failing to stop his car as requested by William Fraser of Toberchurn, while Fraser was driving a horse and dog cart.

Torvaig and Torwell
Two houses are shown as Torvaig on the 1:25,000 OS 1986 sheet, one at NH64676392 and the other close by at NH64986419. This arose as Don Ross, for whom the original Torvaig was built, took the name with him when he moved to the farmhouse at the old Post Office site.

The buildings at NH64676392 were for many years the location of the Post Office in Cullicudden. In the 1870s, Cullicudden Post Office was described thus: *"This is a minor office, subject to Invergordon, to which the mail bag is conveyed, by a travelling postman... The dwelling house is one storey high, thatched and in good repair."* The Post Office and shop were housed in the annexe to the east, with a further smaller east annexe housing farmworkers.

In the early 1900s, John McKenzie, known as *"Jock Sheem,"* from Gairloch, was *"Sub Postmaster General."* Mrs Christina (*"Big Teen"*) McKenzie ms Fraser ran the Post Office and shop into the 1920s, and her niece Mrs Katie Jane Munro ms Fraser and husband William took it over. Mrs Munro retired in 1947, and the Post Office moved east to Achmonie, the telephone (which had originally been

in a section of the Post Office), following to its familiar location outside
Achmonie in 1952.

The original Torvaig was renamed Torwell in the late 20th century, an
appropriate name as the well here (to the north of the house itself) was important
as it did not dry up in the summer. Paths to this well can be seen on early OS
mapping. One path was from Achmonie (where the supply did dry up in
summer) as the MacDonald family had permission to obtain water for home and
livestock from this well.

Udale Bay

RSPB information states that Nigg and Udale Bay Nature Reserve is a 1,270 ha
reserve mostly comprising intertidal mudflats with small areas of saltmarsh and
grassland also present. A hide is located at Udale Bay. The Cromarty Firth is
internationally important for wintering wildfowl and waders. At peak times it
may hold over 30,000 birds including 10,000 wigeon. It also supports
internationally important numbers of Icelandic greylag goose and bar-tailed
godwit and nationally important numbers of pintail, scaup, red-breasted
merganser, curlew and redshank.

Evidence of fish traps (both yares and stake nets) is found in the Cromarty
Firth. Both Newhall and Poyntzfield Estates used stake nets. Poyntzfield had a
yare in which was caught "*herring-fry, salmon, and salmon-trout, as well as the
cuttle-fish.*" There are in the National Archives a set of 1851 plans of Udale Bay
used in a dispute about stake net salmon fishing boundaries between Sir George
Gun Munro of Poyntzfield, on the one side, and Mrs Catherine Ross of Cromarty
and Mr William Hogarth (tacksman of Cromarty fishings), on the other. More
recently, many poles were also erected in Udale Bay (as elsewhere) to prevent
enemy flying-boats landing and were left to rot in place.

There is a record of a landing place in Udale Bay, at NH711651, near where
Gordonsmills Burn enters the sea.

Upperwood – Cairn; Kerb (Possible) Scheduled   NH713631

The name of Upperwood (the site at NH713632) dates from at least the 1870s,
when recorded in the OS Name Book. The cairn referred to is described as being
situated 940 m south east of Poyntzfield Mills, has been reduced to a low stony
mound measuring about 23 m in diameter. There are three possible kerb-stones
on the east. It is considered undoubtedly the remains of a prehistoric cairn,
although there is no evidence that it was chambered. A pear-shaped flake scraper
"*with steep retouch along long edge of ventral side,*" 48 mm long, was also
found at NH714636 and was donated to Inverness Museum in 1996.

Whiskypark   NH703656

This was a sizeable farmstead, immediately to the west of the access road to

Gordon's Mill. The first edition OS shows one unroofed and three roofed buildings and a horse-gang. Walker states there was a still here. Only the rubble of Whiskypark remains today, although once it held farming families, including Camerons. A stone in Kirkmichael states: "*Sacred to the memory of Kenneth Cameron, who died at Whisky Park 16th Febry 1875 / 'He was a good man / Volumes could say no more.*'"

Windyridge or Hawthorn Cottage   NH68486603
Named by H D Fraser, the Windyridge name appears on the Valuation Roll for the first time in 1950, previously being known as Hawthorn Cottage. At time of writing, an old hawthorn tree is still present.

Woodbine   NH66496468
Another botanical name of recent origin, Woodbine appears on the Valuation Roll for the first time in 1923/4, although its use on a Cullicudden gravestone suggests it may have been named earlier than this.

Woodhead   NH64726095
In 1567 John (Leslie) bishop of Ross granted to William Leslie of Balquhan (his brother) various lands including "*Wodheid.*" Woodhead is subsequently amongst land passing from the Bishop of Ross to the Urquharts. A 1608 sasine of Thomas Urquhart for various lands in Resolis includes Woodhead. Thereafter, families who held Woodhead included Fraser of Brea, the Gordons of Newhall and the McKenzies of Avoch.

A long-established farm, with much archaeological interest nearby. There is a Scheduled long cairn at NH653607, now accessible following forestry felling, 600 m east south east of Woodhead farmhouse. It measures about 45 m from east to west by about 14 m transversely and is 1.4 m in height. It has been robbed on the north side. Close by at NH650610 there lie the Scheduled wasted remains of what is probably a round Orkney-Cromarty cairn (page 36) measuring about 24.5 m in diameter, standing 330 m east north east of Woodhead farmhouse. On the north there are the massive slabs of a chamber measuring at least 3.7 m from north east to south west by 1.7 m transversely; the entrance-passage is on the north east. This is probably the "*barrow or cairn*" excavated by Sir Alexander McKenzie of Avoch in which "*human bones of immense size*" were found about 1816. At NH646606, about 280 m south south west of Woodhead farmhouse, there is a cairn measuring about 14 m in diameter and 1.3 m in height.

Woodside   NH68736485
Described in the 1870s thus: "*This name applies to a row of workmen's dwelling houses, which are one story high, thatched, and in fair order. Newhall Estate.*"

SOURCES AND REFERENCES

The main sources of the material in this book are:

published standard sources such as newspapers; the Scottish Acts; Register of the Privy Seal; Fasti; Origines Parochiales Scotiae; Calendar of Scottish Supplications to Rome; Ordnance Survey mapping; the websites of Historic Scotland, Scottish Natural Heritage, the Highland Council and the Royal Commission on the Ancient and Historic Monuments of Scotland [RCAHMS];

unpublished records held in the Aberdeen University Library Archives; Archives of the RCAHMS; Cromarty Courthouse; Highland Regional Archives, Inverness; National Archives of Scotland, Edinburgh; Public Record Office, Kew; the National Library of Scotland, Edinburgh; the Ordnance Survey Name Book (OSNB) compiled 1871-1875; and

information provided by the people of Resolis, and those connected with the parish, including Greta Forbes, Sunnylea; Catriona Gillies, North Kessock; James Holm, Ferryton; my late father and mother, Duncan and Isabella Mackay, Alness Ferry; Alistair Matheson, Bog of Cullicudden; Essie Munro, Alness Ferry; the late *"Jean"* Jane Ann Munro, Balblair; Rebecca Ramsay, Newhall House; Kenneth Urquhart, New Orleans; and many, many more.

Publications containing specific Resolis interest include the following.

Alston, David (1999) Ross and Cromarty A Historical Guide. Birlinn Limited.

Alston, David (1996) The Resolis Riot 28th September 1843 and The Jail Break at Cromarty to release Margaret Cameron, one of the rioters. Cromarty Courthouse.

Arthur, The Reverend Robert (1792) Old Statistical Account – Resolis. [Now available electronically on the internet.]

Ash, Marinell (1991) This Noble Harbour. A History of the Cromarty Firth. Cromarty Firth Port Authority.

Baldwin, John R. (editor) (1986) Firthlands of Ross and Sutherland. Scottish Society for Northern Studies.

Beaton, Angus J. (1985) Illustrated Guide to Fortrose and Vicinity, with an appendix on the Antiquities of the Black Isle and a Map.

Beaton, Elizabeth (1992) Ross & Cromarty. An Illustrated Architectural Guide. Royal Incorporation of Architects in Scotland.

Bulloch, John Malcolm (1906) The Families of Gordon of Invergordon, Newhall, also Ardoch, Ross-shire, and Carrol, Sutherland. Dingwall: Ross-shire Printing & Publishing Co.

Close-Brooks, Joanna (1995) The Highlands [RCAHMS Guide]. HMSO.

Cowan, Ian B. (1967) The Parishes of Medieval Scotland. Scottish Record Society Vol. 93.

Gifford, John (1992) The Buildings of Scotland. Highlands and Islands. Penguin Books in association with The Buildings of Scotland Trust.

Gostwick, Martin (editor) (1997) A Noble Smuggler and other stories. Cromarty: Martin Gostwick.

Macgill, William (1909) Old Ross-shire and Scotland as Seen in the Tain and Balnagown Documents. Inverness: The Northern Counties Newspaper and Printing and Publishing Company, Limited. (Supplementary volume 1911).

Mackay, James M. (2003) A Short History of Kirkmichael. Kirkmichael Trust.

Mackay, James M. (2003) The trial of Robert Ferguson for the Murder of Captain Charles Munro, Resolis 1812. In Clan Munro Magazine 23 11-17.

Mackay, James M. (2007) Who put the Poyntz in Poyntzfield? In Clan Munro Magazine 25 38-45.

Malcolm, Eric H. (1993) The Cromarty and Dingwall Light Railway. Cromarty Courthouse.

Meldrum, Edward (1979) The Black Isle Local History and Archaeology Guidebook No. 3.

Miller, Hugh (1835) Scenes and Legends of the North of Scotland; or, The Traditional History of Scotland. Edinburgh: A. & C. Black. [Many editions/reprints.]

Miller, Hugh (1854) My Schools and Schoolmasters; or, The Story of my Education. Edinburgh: Johnstone and Hunter. [Many editions/reprints.]

Mitchell, Sir Arthur (editor) (1906-1908) The Macfarlane Geographical Collections, in 3 volumes. Edinburgh: Publications of The Scottish History Society, first series, Volumes 51-53. Edited from Macfarlane's Transcript in the Advocates' Library.

Mowat, Ian (1981) Easter Ross: The Double Frontier. John Donald.

Reed, David (1995) The excavation of a cemetery and putative chapel site at Newhall Point, Balblair, Ross & Cromarty, 1985. In Proceedings of the Society of Antiquaries of Scotland 125 779-791.

Sage, The Reverend Donald (written 1836; published 1845) New Statistical Account – Resolis. [Now available electronically on the internet].

Sage, The Reverend Donald (1899) Memorabilia Domestica or Parish Life in the North of Scotland. William Rae.

Scottish Vernacular Buildings Working Group. Easter-Ross Conference 1989. Proceedings. No publication details.

Shaw of Tordarroch, Major C.J. (1983) A History of Clan Shaw. Phillimore & Co. Ltd.

Tayler, Henrietta (1946) History of the Family of Urquhart. Aberdeen University Press.

Uncles, Christopher J. (1998) Easter Ross and the Black Isle. Stenlake Publishing.

Walker, The Reverend George S.M. (1958) The Parish of Resolis. Published by the author at Resolis in aid of the War Memorial Hall.

Watson, William John (1904) Place-names of Ross and Cromarty. Inverness: The Northern Counties Printing and Publishing Company, Limited. (Also Ross & Cromarty Heritage Society reprint, 1976; Highland Heritage Books, 1996).

Willis, Douglas (1989) Discovering the Black Isle. John Donald Publishers Ltd.

Woodham, Anthony A. (1954-1956) A survey of prehistoric monuments in the Black Isle. In Proceedings of the Society of Antiquaries of Scotland 65-93.